Advanced Praise for Relationship Ready

"I was amazed before I was halfway through. The insights pierced an arrow into the center of my heart. The wisdom, love and self-awareness in Relationship Ready is unmatched in the otherwise woman-blaming world of relationship advice."
– Ciara Pressler, Author of Game Plan: Achieve Your Goals in Live, Career, and Business

"Heidi Busche is a fireball and inspiration. She speaks from the heart about her journey, and her experience in navigating the world of relationships. What Heidi offers, with humility and grace, is the power of choosing our destiny."
– Rosie Acosta, Founder of Radically Loved Health + Wellness

"As a TV host and radio personality, I've seen my share of relationship experts! Heidi has been a regular contributor to our show for just about a year, and her advice about dating and relationships is as good as any I've heard. Refreshing, honest and funny, Relationship ready should be among your go-to's for advice on how to prepare for the journey toward true love."
– Tra'Renee Chambers, Emmy Award -Winning Television Personality and Radio DJ

"Authentic, entertaining, and honest—*Relationship Ready* is a MUST READ not only for those seeking a relationship, but for anyone committed to being a better, more connected partner in their current relationship. I've been happily married for 9 years and gained new insight into my relationship patterns through this book! I couldn't put it down!"
– Lindsey Schwartz, Founder Powerhouse Women Event

"This book is a must read! I love Heidi's approach to being so authentic, sharing her truth, talking about the realities of dating, making it funny, digestible and helpful to the reader. I love even more though that you can feel Heidi's personal growth and elevation pop from the pages - what worked once, won't work for her now and to read how she's stepped into the now is incredible powerful and admirable. Just invite me to the wedding!"
– Nicole Myden, Founder of the PR Concierge

"Relatable AF"
– Karey Northington, IFBB Pro, Owner of *PROTEINHOUSE* Gilbert, AZ

Heidi Busche

Relationship Ready

How I Stopped Fucking Randos and Started Cupcaking My Soulmate

Heidi Busche

DEDICATION

To my sweet, sweet, loving and supportive husband, who has never wavered and has believed in me enough for the both of us.

To my mother, who took so many phone calls from me for so long.

To my girl gang, the women who chase their dreams; leaving me energized, inspired and joyful.

To all the randos that caused me pain, so that I could become the woman I was destined to be.

CONTENTS

ACKNOWLEDGMENTS

It literally required an entire team of people to help me complete this project and, frankly, a list of thank you's doesn't quite seem sufficient. But here we go! Thank you Karey Northington, for providing accountability and encouragement from the very beginning. Thank you Ciara Pressler, for your incredible insight and guidance into the publishing and promotion process. A huge thank you to Rosie Acosta for helping me launch into an entirely different spiritual plane for the next step of this work. Thank you to Marisa La Fata for use of your laptop during a particularly difficult fight I was having with compatibility between Google Docs and Microsoft Word. Thank you to Sandy Hammer, Liz Allen, Nicole Myden, Lindsey Schwartz, Tra'Renee Chambers, Alec Wilson, Sarah D'Onofrio, Marissa Johnson, Kimberly Oda, Bonnie Lerner and Sonja Synak for all the inspiration, love and support.

INTRODUCTION

If you're still interested in casually dating, friends with benefit-ing, or fucking randos,[1] then you really aren't ready for this book. You know that wobbly table you've got? For now, put this book under the short leg of that table to steady the wobble. Put it on a shelf, bury it in your closet, use it as a coaster. But keep it around for that moment when you realize that you want a relationship and that you have no fucking idea how to make that happen. For the day you realize you've been ready for a relationship for a while now, but you keep dating guys who aren't. For the day when you are horrified to discover that your relationship patterns, the only ones you know, have been hurting you instead of helping you. Then, go grab this book from under the wobbly table, pull it down from the shelf, dig it out of your closet, take last night's half-full water glass off of it. Now, you're ready. Because this book is for women who are ready to have a relationship with an available partner and we've got work to do.

---

[1] I am definitely not here to rando-shame. If you keep reading, you'll see, I've fucked plenty of randos. Sometimes it felt good and sometimes it felt bad. But at the end of the day, I was never as empowered by it as I thought I would be.

First - Some Definitions

What about cupcaking? What is it? Cupcaking isn't some hot new sex thing. Cupcaking that part of your relationship when you are just so into someone that all you want to do is spend time with them. You want to call out of work to lay in bed together all day, you start ranting and raving about how there should be federally-mandated cupcaking leave (akin to FMLA), you want to go grocery shopping and run stupid errands together, you want to stay up late watching movies or listening to records or running trails or whatever your thing is *together*. You wanna spend every blissful minute by each other's side. Like, if you could crawl up into this person's armpit and just snuggle there you would. You want to *cupcake*, ya feel me?

And what about a soulmate? You don't need me to give you a dictionary definition of a soulmate - you can ask Alexa for that. I consider a soulmate to be a partner with whom I can completely be myself. A partner with whom I can establish and maintain a resilient and reciprocal relationship. A partner who will meet me where I'm at and help me to grow into the most authentic version of myself. I think that we can have more than one soulmate over the course of our lives. And because I have plenty of women in my life who I consider soul sisters, I don't believe that all of my life's soulmates are romantic partners.

I never knew how to "do" relationships. I think it's a common misconception that we're born completely ready to show up authentically in our romantic relationships. I certainly wasn't. Over and over I found myself engaging in behaviors that were keeping me from finding a sustainable, romantic relationship. I spent my twenties and most of my thirties dating men who were unavailable in every possible sense of the word. I would have benefitted from reading a book like this, but I also know that we can't hear some of this stuff until we are really ready to hear it. So, as a twenty-something, I could have read this book, comprehended it, completed the exercises and the writing. But, until I was sick and tired of hurting myself with my behavior around relationships; until I was really ready to try something different, it wouldn't have been effective.

I have done all the stuff that I am going to ask you to do; completed all the thought exercises and all of the writing. Doing that work was the price of admission to a life where I know who I am. I am clear about what I want. And I am capable of authentic, sustainable relationships.

In Relationship Ready, I outline the exercises I did to change my relationship patterns with men. Before we jump into that soul-level work, I'll spend some time sharing my story with you. I want you to know, I understand the pain of these patterns, and I hope that some of my experiences resonate with you. Also, with a little distance from them, I can laugh at myself and I hope you can, too. I'm going to be vulnerable with you and I hope you can be just as vulnerable, honest and authentic with me (when you are doing the exercises and the work that comes later).

After we've taken the first four chapters to get to know each other, I'll outline the work you'll need to do to become relationship-ready. Please don't just skip right to (or past) the exercises. I want you to have all the context and information that each chapter provides for each exercise. If you are familiar with twelve-step recovery work, then some of the exercises will, undoubtedly, be familiar. I initially did this work with a woman that I knew from a twelve-step program of recovery. But when I finished it, I realized that so many women who might never be exposed to twelve-step recovery could benefit from this work. And so I have modified it, and present it here. Like so many of the constructs that we use in the process of self-discovery, self-help, and therapy, the tools here are derivative from time-tested concepts.

Chapter 5 is the first chapter that will require some action on your part. It delivers clear direction on how to get the most out of this. I'll tell you right now, I'm going to ask you to put some distance between yourself and the people that you're flirting with or dating. A gentle reminder, the purpose of this work is to become relationship ready.

Chapters 6, 7, and 8 will provide the framework for the bulk of the writing to be done. In these chapters, you are going to identify the patterns in relationships that are causing you pain. You'll likely know some of these when you start, but I guarantee you will uncover some patterns that you didn't know were driving your behavior. You'll also have the opportunity to explore your fears around relationships. And I'll provide some concrete actions you can take around both the patterns and fears, no matter what they are.

Chapters 9, 10, and 11 are about forgiving yourself, changing these behaviors, and learning how to do something different. I've got tools and exercises in these chapters for building your girl-gang, for identifying your ideal partner, and letting all the old stuff go. Finally, in Chapters 12 and 13, I give you some guidelines for dating and I talk about how I met the love of my life, Mr. Husband.

This work is simple, but it's not easy; nothing worthwhile ever is. All my life, I thought, "true love and intimacy are for other people - the beautiful people - not for me." Honestly, for as long as I can remember, I thought this was true. With this work, I changed my perspective, I shredded the old narrative, and I started to believe: "Anything that I want can be mine. I am worthy." No matter what your old, limiting beliefs, this work can help you set them aside. We are not meant to do this alone, we are not meant to be fearful, miserable, or angry. I truly believe that we are all meant to shine; that an authentic life with deep intimacy is possible for each and every one of us. This work has provided it for me and I know it can provide it for you too.

Xoxo to the maxxxxx.

HB

1

I JUST WANNA BE WALLPAPER

Who am I?

What makes me an expert?

Why would you want to take my advice when it comes to your love life?

I get it, we've never met, and we don't know anything about each other. One of the most beautiful things that I'm learning about being human is, the power of shared experience. And, I believe that if I share my journey to love with you, at some stage along the way, you'll smile and say to yourself, "Holy shit. I've done that, too."   Anytime I get to hear another woman share her story about her path to love, I am reminded: I am not alone. I am not special or unique. I am not bad, and I am not beyond help. I am just a spiritual being having a human experience.

I decided to embark on this soul-level work with another woman in my life, Ms. Warrior Spirit. Sharing my feelings, my innermost narrative, and my experiences with her was transformational. And, it deepened my connection to her, to a myriad of other women in the world and, perhaps most importantly, to myself. I was not always this way; deep connection is not my factory default setting.

I grew up in Iowa, just west of the Mississippi River. I was such an uncomfortable kid. We moved to Iowa the summer before I began the second grade and I always felt like an outsider there. I was shy. Painfully shy. I was so scared to be me. I was terrified to try to make new friends, and it always felt like I was doing it wrong. I remember I would just sit around and hope that, like, the wallpaper would absorb me. I dreamt of being a chameleon so that I could just be camouflaged by my surroundings.

I'll admit, it's strange to write that because it is so different from the woman that I am today. But, that shyness, that desire to blend into nothingness, to become oblivion, still creeps up for me. I meet a lot of people and, occasionally, even if I've met you and we know each other, I will assume that you don't remember me. I assume that I'm wallpaper to people. I assume that there's no way that anyone will ever remember my face. In the old days, I believed that narrative, and so I would slink and shy away from people. But today, I try to take contrary action around it. So, I do my best to be as outgoing as possible (no matter how awkward it is) and to remember that I'm probably not the only person who has ever felt like wallpaper or who wanted to disappear.

Ok - so what does any of this have to do with my love life?! My formative years and early relationships were molded by this narrative of "outsider-ness." In preparing for this chapter and this book, I reflected on some of these early experiences with boys and three, in particular, sum them up.

My First Boyfriend

I was a sixth grader at Bettendorf Middle School when I opened my little yellow locker one day and found a note. OMG. This was not a note from my best friend Krissy Samuels.[2] No, this was a note from a boy. Well kind of. It was actually a note from another girl on behalf of a boy. BOOM. Be still my beating heart. I had seen Saved by the Bell, I had watched Beverly Hills 90210, I was prepared. I knew what I was supposed to do.

---

[2] For Christmas that year, my Aunt Marti had gifted me several print copies of the Onion. Krissy and I had decided that our middle school needed its own Onion and so, the Pathological Press was born. We'd spent the entire year passing notes and curating its news.

I grabbed the note. Shut my locker. Held my notebook tight to my chest. I leaned back on my heels and swiveled around (so that my back was to my locker and my face was toward the hallway) and I rested (casually, very casually) back on my locker door as I read the note. Melissa was asking me - via this note - (a) if I thought that Brad Paulson was cute and (b) if I wanted to go out with him. I thought I was going to jump out of my skin. Did I want to go out with Brad Paulson?? Abso-fucking-lutely. Did I think Brad was cute? I couldn't tell you; I had no idea who Brad was. But that was only a minor detail, right? Surely, I could say yes to this offer and get to know Brad. And did it really matter? Wasn't everything in life about who a person was, rather than what they looked like? Yes, Melissa, yes, I would be happy to "go out with" Brad. That would be great. Thank you very much.

I was so excited to be going out with a boy in my class. I felt like I was doing things right and finally, finally fitting in. Two days later, Jessie came by my locker. She cornered me, and in that sixth-grade-girl-kind-of-way, said, "Heidi, are you going out with Brad?"

I confidently replied, "Yep." I smiled, I was, after all, ready to ride or die for my new boo.

But she threw her head back and laughed. And then she said "Ewwwww."

And that was all it took. The shame spiral was real, and it was deep. I should have known better. How could I have believed that I was worthy of Kelly Kapowski - Zach Morris love? How stupid was I to think, even for a second, (for two whole days no less), that that kind of love was for me? That kind of love was for other people. Beautiful people. People who belonged, and who mattered and who knew how to live a good, Midwestern life.

This was a powerful turning point for me. Because, although it was not my first heartbreak, it was my first experience of doubting myself, my first experience of seeking the validation of others. If Jessie had a different reaction, I might have continued to go out with Brad. Jessie wasn't a good friend of mine. She wasn't a girl that I spent a lot of time with, or whose opinion I trusted. But, for some reason, her assessment of what I was doing mattered to sixth-grade me.

After the Brad Paulson debacle, I had some crushes and did a little bit of flirting, but I just never felt comfortable putting myself out there. And I really didn't want to put myself out there with anyone that anyone at school knew. Sometimes, I flirted with boys who didn't go to my school, boys I met through community sports programs, or sons of family friends, but decided that the boys at my school were

> I should have known better. How could I have believed that I was worthy of Kelly Kapowski - Zach Morris love?

strictly off limits. Boys who were available to me were dangerous—they could make me look stupid, like I didn't know what I was doing. And yet, at the same time, the thought of dating them also seemed quite pedestrian. Wouldn't it be more exciting if I liked someone who I didn't see every day? Wasn't that kind of "love" more exotic?

My First (Real) Boyfriend

But the last segment was titled, My First Boyfriend! Yes, but this is the story of my first real boyfriend. I was fourteen and I signed up to spend a week in Americus, Georgia, building homes for Habitat for Humanity. I was afforded this incredible experience by First Presbyterian Church of Davenport (an unlikely and surprisingly comfortable spot for fourteen-year-old me).

Our little youth group met up with another little youth group from a different part of the state and boarded a chartered bus headed to Georgia. A quick disclaimer: I can't even begin to tell you the disdain that the words "church youth group" conjure up for me *in spite* of the fact that I had a wonderful, supportive, inclusive, experience as a member of a church youth group in Iowa. So please, for this little vignette, I encourage you to set aside any prejudice that those words might bring up for you and to, instead, envision us as this little gang of misfits. Heading to Georgia. On a bus. From Iowa. To build houses.

When you're a kid, there is nothing like a trip without your parents, right? The excitement and overwhelm of getting on the bus. The rush to get a seat near the back. Taking inventory and checking everyone out: who's a jock, who's a nerd, who's a bitch, who is the cute-cool-laid-back-girl, who is the guy-with-a-soft-sensitive-side? Which one am I? Who will I be? No one here knows me; I can be whoever I want! Or better yet, I can be whoever they will like best!! And I will fit. I will fit in.

I spent the entire week flirting with Tom. Tom lived an hour away from me in our real lives. I felt the rush of young love, young lust, and it was exhilarating. We bussed home and parting ways was so dramatic. Would I ever see Tom again? How could my life possibly go on without him?

Well, I did see Tom again. Tom and I talked on the phone. OMG, did we talk on the phone. And our flirtation was filled with a ton of fantasy.

"I can't wait to take you to my favorite bowling alley." Tom was a very good bowler.

"Won't it be great when we are older, and we can go to a fancy dinner?" It sure would beat a bowling alley.

And, honestly, I have no idea what my parents were thinking, but they drove me to see him. And his parents let me stay at his house. And then his parents drove him to see me and my parents let him stay at our house. And even typing this out, twenty years later, sounds totally and completely insane. This young love eventually ran its course. But it was exhilarating. When would he call? When would I be able to call him? When would I see him next? How would we get to one another? There was so little reality to our flirtation and our interactions. But of course, I couldn't see that at the time. Today I think about this and I have some compassion for fourteen-year-old me, it's like, you don't know what you don't know, you know? At the time this felt like excitement, not heartbreak. At the time, I didn't think that it was the beginning of a painful pattern of becoming involved with unavailable men. At the time, I just thought it was fun.

Teenagers are delusional about a lot of things, not the least of which is love. But here I was, at fourteen years old, already climbing in my own little car on the unavailability roller coaster. Already checking to make sure that my shoulder harness was pulled down tight with delighted anticipation for each click, click, click that the roller coaster made on its way up for the big drop. Looking back on it, it's like I skipped the kid version of this ride (you know the little, elephants that just go around in a circle on the rails) and went straight for the ride that has two loops and a death-defying drop. I know this was my first experience reveling in the fantasy of unavailability.

The Advent of the Internet

Some of you will recall a time when the internet did not exist. Without launching into a nostalgic soliloquy about the days without instant gratification, I will just say this: there was a time when you could not just dial up a man's attention. When you couldn't open an app to see how many of your photos he liked; when you didn't monitor your phone constantly to see how many men had commented on how great your legs looked in that skirt.

I was about sixteen when AOL made chatrooms widely available to anyone who had a dial-up modem. There were some drawbacks. First, connections weren't always reliable, so on any day you might get kicked off or bounced out mid-chat/flirt. Second, in my house, the computer was in my dad's home office, which doubled as a Lego room for my brother. So, navigating a Lego minefield was the price I paid to chat, anonymously, with strange men online (#totallyworthit). Third, we only had one phone line in our house, so time spent online had to be negotiated with my parents - which I credit, to this day, for my superb negotiating skills.

AOL chat rooms were incredible because, in them, no one knew anything about anyone else. Obviously, this makes them dangerous and a natural place for predatory behavior. And I probably understood that at the time. But I didn't care. Because when I was Unntz218@aol.com, I could be whoever I wanted to be or more importantly (as I was discovering) whoever you wanted me to be.

The other thing that I loved about them, was that no one really had to know what I looked like. I was a heavy kid with low self-esteem. It was infinitely easier for me to talk to people while I was hiding behind a screen name. I could say what I wanted. I felt like in this anonymous place—where everyone was unavailable and the truth was what you made it—I could be vulnerable, it was safe to try on a new personality, it was as easy to say things I didn't mean as it was to say things that I did.

So, navigating a Lego minefield was the price I paid to chat, anonymously, with strange men online (#totallyworthit).

When I was eighteen, I had just finished my freshman year at the University of Pittsburgh, and I was back home in Iowa for the summer. I was kind of reconnecting with a guy I had dated in high school when I met a guy online, Darren. Darren lived in Pittsburgh and was maybe a few years older than me. I spent *hours* chatting with him that summer. Eventually, he invited me to visit him. I did. Which wasn't a big deal.

The lie that I told my parents - I mean - I'd put that in the "big deal" category. That summer, while most of my friends were "lifeguarding" at Wacky Waters,[3] I was spending my afternoons and evenings working as a hostess in a Cheddars Restaurant. I liked it because I was almost always done by 10 p.m. and I never had to be in much earlier than 10 a.m. I was never in the hot sun. I always got a discount on a meal, and even though the servers had to wear shirts and ties, I only had to wear a button-down shirt and khakis. I was sometimes jealous of the servers (because hello, money). But they treated me like they knew I was a good kid and that they thought I was going places. They were protective, they were kind, they were tremendously patient, and sometimes they bought me booze. And that felt good.

---

[3] Read: getting stoned and laying in the sun.

I didn't have the money to fly to Pittsburgh to meet my internet love. I needed my parents to fly me there. They didn't know that I was talking to a stranger on the internet. And although they had been so understanding around my first long-distance relationship with Mr. Habitat for Humanity, I did not think they would find this as, hmmm, shall we say, cute. I told them that I was heading to Pittsburgh to visit my friends from college and that I would be staying with them on campus. And they agreed to buy me a ticket. Instead, I flew into Pittsburgh, met this man I had been chatting with online, stayed in a hotel room with him and threw myself into the fantasy of this long-distance "relationship."

I was lucky that, despite my recklessness, I did not get hurt or assaulted by Darren. That he turned out to be a nice, pretty well-adjusted young man in his early twenties. I look back on this experience with tremendous gratitude that I emerged from it unscathed.

During these years I did not find sustainable, meaningful, or emotionally fulfilling relationships. Shocker, I know. I did, however, discover the lengths I was willing to go to in the pursuit of fantasy, unavailable men, and male attention. I had put myself in danger. And I hadn't even thought twice about it, I didn't even blink. If you had asked me then, would I do it again, the answer would have been "Absolutely!" The attention of men was a powerful drug to me. It took me places I never thought I would go, I found myself doing things I never thought I'd do. The price of admission was my integrity and my true self. Things had to get worse before they got better for me. I rode the roller-coaster throughout most of my adult life, but it ratcheted up a notch when I hit my early twenties, and that's the part of my story I want to share with you next.

2

THE COLLEGE YEARS

I couldn't wait to get out of Iowa. So, I sent all of my college applications to out-of-state schools and I was delighted when I was accepted to the University of Pittsburgh. I was headed to the East Coast![4]

Anyway, you know that even before I even left for the University of Pittsburgh, I had already developed some unhealthy patterns around men and relationships. I was smitten by men who were not geographically available to me, I was obsessed with the fantasy of a long-distance relationship. Flirting with men who didn't live near me or know anything about me allowed me to create interactions and relationships that were never grounded in reality. This was appealing to me for a number of reasons.

First, there was the rush of flirting with someone new; someone completely unknown. You know this feeling; sending lots of messages, anticipating the response, starting with cutie emoticons (and eventually emojis) and slowly working toward more salacious chat. So, there was a sense of both immediate and delayed gratification. Immediately gratifying in the sense

---

[4] I get it, Pittsburgh is only considered the East Coast if you're from the Midwest. And it's considered the Midwest by anyone who actually lives on the East Coast. But I digress.

that, without overthinking it or giving it much thought at all, I could just crank out a message. I could just start typing or texting away and I got to say things to men that I could or would never say in real life. I could be skanky and vulnerable. I could hide behind a screen, and it felt good.

Messaging and its attendant delayed gratification was both torturous (in the best way) and thrilling. When I was texting smutty and sexy stuff, I wondered, *Did I go too far? Did I shock him? Did he think it was hot?* When I was being vulnerable it was more along the lines of; *Did he feel sorry for me and my tragic life? Did I explain that right? Did I send one message to many?!?!*

Second, I didn't have to be me. I was ashamed of me, I was embarrassed of me, I felt like 'me' didn't know how to do any of this relationship or sex stuff "right." At that time, it was appealing, no, it was amazing, to have the space to be less like me and more like whatever whoever I was talking to wanted me to be. Did I wanna try being a straight-edge kid? Just added an "x" to the front and back of my screen name and voila, Unntz218@aol.com became xUnntz218x@aol.com and I was as edgy or as straight as need be.

Third, I felt safe. I had some fresh abandonment wounds (I'll definitely get to those in the next few chapters) and dating in this way allowed me to feel like I was in control. As cliché as it sounds, it allowed me to keep people just far enough away so that they couldn't hurt my heart.

I was smitten by men who were not geographically available to me, I was obsessed with the fantasy of a long-distance relationship. Flirting with men who didn't live near me or know anything about me allowed me to create interactions and relationships that were never grounded in reality.

But the thing that really made long-distance flirtation or relationships a *fantasy* for me was the actual interaction. I would much rather drop into someone's life for the weekend than actually *live* life with them. It was infinitely easier to hop on a plane, fly to a different city, do some sightseeing, and eat out each night, than to run errands and, like, buy baby carrots together. The problem, of course, with this fantasy life, is that it is not conducive to sustainable, long-term relationships. So, my heart was saying, "I want a boyfriend, I want to have a long-term relationship with someone who 'gets' me," but my actions were saying, "I want a fling!"

I spent the first year or two of college chasing the long-distance fantasy—mostly by clinging onto a relationship I had with Mr. Highschool. By my junior year of high school, I had set my sights on a group of guys that I wanted to roll with. They were smart and funny, and like swimming and cross-country jocks, so not actual jocks, but still hot and in shape. They were safely a year ahead of me, but we had a lot of AP classes together. So, I assessed the group. Who was the most accessible? Who could give me access to this group and, yet, not require that I actually put my heart out there? Mr. Highschool, that's who.

Mr. Highschool and I got along, but our relationship was one of convenience. And we kind of just rolled that way for a couple of years, never really rocking the boat, never really wading into "too-serious" territory. My dating him giving me access to his social crew and him dating me giving him access to, well, me. We partied together and as we grew up; we would hang out when he was back from school or when we were both back from school. But we never really had a deep commitment to or connection with one another.

Dating Mr. Highschool was the first time that I started to use men for access. It was the first time that I realized dating the "right" guy might put me in the middle of a whole new crew. And maybe if I played my cards right, I could trade up. It's ugly, it makes me cringe, but it's true, and I know that I'm not the only woman in the world who has done this (and I'm certainly not the only sixteen-year-old that ever did).

When Mr. Highschool and I went to colleges in different states, instead of breaking up for good, we still kind of hung on to one another. We were both members of Greek Letter organizations. And Greek formals and date events gave us opportunities to swoop in and out of one another's lives. Some weekends were magical, some weekends were … not. During one weekend, I flew into Denver to attend a fraternity formal with Mr.

Highschool. We drove to some ski resort with all of his fraternity brothers and I got loaded at the event. I insisted on blowing him in the shower that night. Generally, I would not recommend this, what with the challenges of sucking a dick, breathing, and adding water to the mix. But on this particular evening, I was glad that was where we ended up. Mid-blow-job, I got so sick, I threw up all over him. It was as awful as it sounds.

You might be saying to yourself, "Jesus Christ, what the fuck, Heidi! What is this story?!?!" Well, frankly, I did want to make sure you were still paying attention. But also to make the point that hanging on to the idea of a long-distance romance with Mr. Highschool, kept me from exploring relationships with any men who were even in the same area code as me. And, honestly, even when I did get physical with men in my area code, neither they nor I were really relationship material. I always selected men who were unavailable. And I often put myself in danger in the process.

I believe that there are three kinds of unavailability (1) he doesn't live near you, (2) he isn't single, (3) he's not emotionally available. My earliest dabbling with unavailable men was with men who didn't live near me. But, as I settled into Pittsburgh, I started chasing a new kind of unavailability. I got really hooked on men who weren't single. Here's how that happened.

By the time I was a Junior, it was the early 2000s; super low-rise jeans, crop tops, and white eyeliner reigned supreme. Christina Aguilera, Britney Spears, Eve and Mary J. Blige topped the charts. Some sorority sisters and I decided to rent a house off campus—a glorious, place on Meyran Avenue in South Oakland at Pitt. If it wasn't condemned before we moved in, it certainly was after we left. That house had four bedrooms and two full bathrooms. Eleven of us lived there. We had lived on campus together already, but there was something about living in this particular house. I guess it was this; when we lived together on campus, there were strict rules at the dorms around boyfriends

> Generally, I would not recommend this, what with the challenges of sucking a dick, breathing, and adding water to the mix.

and visitors. When we moved off campus, all hell broke loose.

A couple of things were happening for me at this time. During these days I was rapidly approaching my first alcoholic bottom; one of several opportunities that I had to get sober, but for which I just wasn't ready. Second, part of the manifestation of my alcoholism is that I always felt like I wasn't "a part of." So, even though I had known most of these women for more than a couple of years, I didn't truly believe that I belonged as a part of their crew.

Third, like I said, I was a heavy (if athletic) kid, with low self-esteem. In the fourth grade, I adopted a "vegetarian" lifestyle where I ate nothing but mac and cheese. I gained about seventy pounds that I held onto for a long time. I don't ever recall wearing small pant sizes in women's clothes, it seemed like overnight that I went from bopping around in kid clothes to being at the top of the size range (I had been at least a size 14 since I was thirteen). It took an excruciating toll on my self-esteem. By my junior year of college, long stretches of day drinking and late-night eating had me rockin' a middle-age "dad-bod." I was tipping the scales at about 200 pounds and I really struggled to find any way to love myself.

My low self-esteem told me that, even if I could roll with these girls, I wasn't like them. I wasn't beautiful. They were beautiful. They wore size 0 and

...there are three kinds of unavailability (1) he doesn't live near you, (2) he isn't single, (3) he's not emotionally available.

00 pants (goddamned fucking double zero!!) and XXS tops. Everything looked cute on them because they were, like, these little elven people. These girls dated athletes and bartenders, drank for free, and it seemed like they lived their lives without consequences. There was nothing that the batting of eyes, a crop top and a giggle couldn't get them out of. The whole time that I lived with them, I heard the narrative that I had been telling myself since I was a sixth-grader. Dating. Relationships. Love. Those things were for them, the beautiful people, not me.

So much of my perception of my life, and the women in it, was distorted by all of the stuff in my head. Distorted by my own self-loathing, distorted by my jealousy, distorted by my sense of entitlement, distorted by my self-pity. The reality is, those girls were humans, just like me. Each struggling with her own baggage, each fighting some battle that I was too self-centered to know anything about. Each of them has walked through fire to be transformed into the woman she is today. And, I can tell you that, it wouldn't have mattered which eleven women I was living with at that stage, I would have had the same feelings. To live through the feelings I was having, to explore them, and grow from them, was a part of my journey. And I have no doubt that the universe would have delivered that journey to me no matter who I was living with. So, I feel extraordinarily lucky to have had some of these ladies in my corner for over fifteen years.

There is one other thing that I need to make abundantly clear: my dysfunction with men and relationships at this stage of my life was absolutely not due to the fact that I was wearing size 16 pants and size XL shirts. It was directly related to my inability to love and value myself. My inability to form sustainable relationships with men had more to do with my sickness and dysfunction around boundaries and availability than with what I looked like. And the only way that I was able to change that dysfunction was to do the work that I've outlined in this book. I repeat: if you are struggling with the things I struggled with and you can identify with the anecdotes in this book, your problem is not what you look like. Your problem is related to a lack of self-worth, a lack of self-love and the manifestation of that in the pursuit of dysfunctional and/or unavailable men. I happen to be thinner today, but I didn't need to lose weight to find love. I firmly believe that love is available to any and all who are seeking it.

So much of growing up and finding my capital-T TRUTH has been related to testing boundaries and leaning into my full self. About reacting to life and sharing my experiences authentically with others. About really coming to believe that I am not "too much" for anyone to handle; that my feelings are valid, no matter what they are. That I am Ok, with or without you.

In a house of eleven twenty-something women, growing up is about drama. And we had no shortage of drama. It didn't matter which girl it was or what drama was going on, I was always there commiserating with her boyfriend. And it comes down to this, I just always thought that while he (whichever "he" it was, Brad, John, Mike Jason, Chuck, Chad, just insert generic dude -

bro name here) and I were commiserating over cleaning up her puke or waiting for her to finally get ready to go out or doing shots at the bar while she flirted with other men, he would look at me. And he would realize that I was amazing and awesome and exactly the down to earth kind of girl he had always been looking for. And he would leave her for me. I was the cool chick friend. You know, the girl who could watch football? The girl who could do a shot of Jack and Jim? The girl who was ready on time and low-maintenance? That was me.

I didn't always pine over my roommates' boyfriends', eventually I pined over men who were involved with other women who weren't my roommates. Which was still the same old shit. One summer, we had a neighbor who lived across the street from us, Mr. EnglishLit. He had a dentist chair in his living room, he was handsome and smart and, of course, he was unavailable. One of the first things that he proclaimed to me was that he and his girlfriend had sex in the dentist chair all the time. Well. I will be goddamned, if I didn't want to have sex in a dentist chair with this guy all the time too. I didn't even know, like, logistically, how that would work, but I knew I wanted it. I knew I wanted him. This guy. I sought and craved his attention as validation, that I felt like in order to exist in the world, I needed this guy to see me. I was so deep in my sickness around relationships, desirability, and love, that I thought I could trick him into being with me or loving me somehow. With this guy and his girlfriend, I just wanted to win.

There was Mr. Youngstown, in his baggy khaki pants and his dumb Timbs. He and his girlfriend were long distance and I am sure she didn't appreciate the way that he and I ran around town. I was always just, I guess, pining for him. I was always poking around, asking what was going on with him and her, sidling up to him with a sympathetic ear, "Ugh, what a biiiitch, man, that sucks. Let's go get some 40s, duct tape them to our hands, and get fucked up! EDWARD 40-HAAANDS!!!" Always wishing, always hoping, he would leave her for me.

So, there was one huge piece of falling for unavailable men that was about winning, that was about romantic comedy fantasy, that was about being underestimated and coming out on top. But it was also about safety. I could be the cool girl, I could always be level-headed and low-maintenance, because none of my shit was on blast. I wasn't taking any risks or being vulnerable. I wasn't testing any of my truth. I wasn't being authentic. I wasn't being honest with myself or anyone else. I was putting on a personality, which was specifically crafted to be more appealing to this guy than the personality of whomever he was dating.

Pretending to be the "cool girl" nearly killed me. It was death by a thousand paper cuts; it caused me more pain than I ever thought possible. Because it required denying everything about myself in order to become everything that other people thought was cool. And at first, it didn't feel too bad to push down a few feelings about this or that for the sake of being "chill." To make shitty jokes at the expense of my friends or throw them under the bus to make their dumb boyfriends laugh, or to get a cool nickname from them. And, honestly, I don't think I realized, at the time how manipulative it was.

I could be the cool girl, I could always be level-headed and low-maintenance, because none of my shit was on blast.

But eventually, I lost myself. Also, it was shitty to always be creeping on my friends' men. I have friends today and women in my life today because I no longer behave this way. And I don't think of love or relationship as games, they aren't about winning or losing out to someone else. Today, it's about finding a deep and meaningful spiritual and emotional connection to another human. But you know what they say? It's all fun and games until you get fucked in the face. Just kidding. Nobody says that. Here's the truth, it took what it took to get there. And for me, it was a lot of shit.

3

SO, YOU WANT TO GET MARRIED

There were a number of reasons why I was unavailable as a romantic partner in my twenties, one of which was my alcoholism. I think that a lot of people have one specific idea of what alcoholism looks like (read: dirty hobo living under a bridge drinking out of a bottle that's in a bag). My alcoholism did not look like that, and yet, it is part of me and my story. I do believe that I was born with the disease of alcoholism. Today I think of it often as a disease of more—more food, more attention, more drinks, more sex, more men, more shopping, more anything. For as long as I can remember, I was always trying to change the way I felt. I was always chasing something, and I was convinced that if I could only find the right "thing" out there, it would help me feel different "in here." And that was what I really wanted: to feel different.

As a kid, I found this solution in food. When I was eight years old, I became completely obsessed with Archway chocolate chip cookies. Every single day, I would walk in the garage door, drop my backpack, head straight to the kitchen, pile three cookies on a plate, pour a glass of milk, turn on the TV, eat the cookies, and feel better. It worked. Every. Single. Time.

Eventually, I replaced this cookie routine with alcohol and for a long time, it also worked for me. Until it didn't. The wheels really came off for the first time, when I was in my early twenties. I had just graduated from college; I was working as the day waitress in a wing-bar called Smokin' Joes on the South Side of Pittsburgh. For about a half hour each day, during the lunch rush, I served wings to, like, five lunch time customers. Then, I spent the rest of the day sitting at the bar, drinking diet RC and reading Charles Bukowski while I counted the minutes until I was done. I made approximately $2.83 in tips each day on top of the $1.56/hour that I earned as a waitress.

I would finish my shift at Smokin' Joes and I would have a shift beer, which would usually turn in to at least six or seven. Then, inevitably, I would insist on going somewhere else; sometimes the corner store to pick up more booze, sometimes a strip club (which in my memory was open 24-7). I would stumble home at 4 a.m. In the morning, I would come to, throw on jeans and a hoodie, grab my apron, Bukowski, and a pack of cigarettes, and head back to work.

> I spent the rest of the day sitting at the bar, drinking diet RC, and reading Charles Bukowski while I counted the minutes until I was done.

I regularly drunk-dialed my mom, and it was one of the most humiliating things I did. At the time, my mom was about four years sober. I called her, shit-faced, two or three times a week. But she always picked up the phone and the next day she would always call me back to make a few simple suggestions. What if today you just stopped beating yourself up? What if today, you made your bed? How about you just take a shower, take a deep breath, have some breakfast, and go to work? Over and over, she would provide this quite-reasonable direction. Sometimes I took her suggestions and other times, I couldn't. On and on we did this dance, until one day, she'd had enough.

What Happened Was

What had happened was, I had finished my shift and I had my shift beer at Smokin' Joes. About twenty beers later, I decided that I should tell Mr. Joe that I hated him, that I hated the bar, that the whole thing was stupid, and that Iowa was better than this. Mr. Joe responded by firing me and telling me that I should actually go back to Iowa. And I concurred, "Faaaaaaaack you." So then I left that place. My dad had bailed me out of some other bullshit[5] so I had about $1,500 in my bank account. I went on a bender; strip clubs, shots, men, booze.

I burned my life to the ground in three days, and then, of course, I called my mom. I don't remember exactly what I told her, but I heard her say, "You can't live in Pittsburgh anymore," and I heard me say, "okay." She said, "I'm coming to get you." I was tired. I was really fucking tired. I was tired of being angry at everyone and everything. I was tired of grinding and grinding and grinding to try to make my life come together. I was tired of doing the same old shit and getting the same old results.

So, my mom and a friend of hers drove eight hours from Iowa to Pittsburgh to extract me from my life and drive me home. This was it. Surely, I was headed to rehab. But she didn't send me anywhere and she didn't make any demands on me. Honestly, I don't remember her even lecturing me. And we drove across the fucking largest state in the union, Ohio.[6] And then through Illinois. And then to Iowa.

We got home and she was like, "Ok, you live here now." Ugh. A fate worse than rehab. Iowa. The first weekend I was home, I decided to drive

---

[5] Bullshit included: being unable to pay my rent, being unable to pay my bills, overdrawing my bank account, run-ins with law enforcement, mouthing off to law enforcement, jumping out of moving law enforcement vehicles. You get the idea.
[6] I mean, that state is just so god-damned big, it never ends. It's like, oh, where are we? Ohio. Five hours later. Hey, what state are we in? Oh, damn. We're still in Ohio. It's like the twilight zone out there.

about 45 min or so to Iowa City (the nearest college town) to party. I hooked up with a guy I knew from high school. He was in Iowa City for the weekend but living in Denver. As we were lying in bed around 4 a.m., he turned to me and said, "If you lived in Denver, I would make you breakfast."

So, you know what I did? The next week, I packed my stuff into my blue Jeep Cherokee, and headed to Denver. Let me make that crystal clear for you. I moved to Denver because a man promised to make me breakfast. I moved. To a different state. Where I didn't know anyone. For some fucking scrambled eggs.[7]

I'm not even sure that I called or texted Mr. Breakfast to him to let him know I was coming. I do remember showing up on his doorstep, like "Here I am, can we have some breakfast now? Oh, and also, I don't have a TV can I borrow yours?" I stayed in his apartment with him and his roommate for weeks. But eventually I found my own spot. I had a mattress and this little TV of his that I had basically stolen. I went to a Costco and stocked my apartment with disposable plates, silverware and cups. Investing in dishes felt like, "Meh, why? What's the point?" It makes me kinda sad and it was so absurd, but honestly, buying dishes, silverware and stuff for my kitchen in Denver just seemed like too much of a commitment. My life there seemed so... transient.

I got a job waiting tables. A few weeks later, I met some girlfriends out for drinks. We had tequila shots. I am 97% sure that this was the last night that I drank tequila. After I had been at this bar for a few hours, a very short guy started talking to me at the bar. He told me that he played football for the Denver Broncos. Imagine that! Me - getting hit on by a football player! This was so exciting. But, actually, it was a little more like: imagine that, me - so drunk, desperate, and lonely, that I thought the 5'2" guy who was hitting on me might actually be a professional football player.

Of course, I took Mr. Football home to my apartment with me (even though I was still involved with Mr. Breakfast). I can remember making out

---

[7] Just in case you're wondering, there are plenty of scrambled eggs in Iowa.

with Mr. Football but I don't remember when we stopped and I don't remember if we did anything else. I have no recollection of what was going on when we stopped making out and I have no idea whether or not I had sex with him.

Let me make that crystal clear for you. I moved to Denver because a man promised to make me breakfast. I moved. To a different state. Where I didn't know anyone. For some fucking scrambled eggs.

I was terrified and horrified when I came to the next morning. It's an interesting mix of feelings that I know many alcoholics are familiar with. The terror is largely the result of the blackout, of losing huge chunks of time, of an awareness that your body was awake and moving, but your brain can't recall what the fuck your body was doing. For me, the terror gets a level-up when my body moving involves another human's body, too. Or when my body moving involves a vehicle. The horror is largely a consequence of the guilt and shame that follows. *How could I have lost that time? What was I thinking eating the entire menu at KenTacoHut? Is the person next to me a serial killer?* You know, just a few run of the mill, morning after, kind of, questions.

I woke up next to Mr. Football. Ugh. What had I done? *Never mind. Never mind.* I told myself. *Just get this guy out of here.* I woke him up, left the bedroom and I waited in the kitchen to give him some privacy. He got dressed and came out and asked if I could take him home. We got in the car and I drove him to some part of Denver.

We were at a busy intersection and he said to me, "It's fine. Just pull over here." I was so mortified, humiliated, embarrassed, and ashamed over my behavior that I practically kicked him out of the car.

I didn't get his name; I didn't take his phone number. Just GTFO.

I got home and discovered that while I had been in the kitchen, giving him some privacy, he had gone from my bedroom into my bathroom, had

25

opened my jewelry box and had stolen every single piece of jewelry I owned. Family heirlooms, gone. Tiffany jewelry, bye. Sentimental stuff, see ya. It was awful. And as I realized I was damn lucky that I wasn't raped, hurt, or murdered, I felt so much shame. Looking back, I know that surviving that night safe and sound had nothing to do with me or my choices; it had nothing to do with my moral character or what I was wearing or what I looked like. I was just fucking lucky.

I called my mom. I called the Denver police. They sent someone to take a report and told me that they would check at pawn shops. But all I could hear was that this was what I deserved for bringing a stranger to my place. The shame was excruciating. I had moved to Denver for scrambled eggs, I had stolen Mr. Breakfast's TV, I was robbed by Mr. Football *plus* I had cheated on Mr. Breakfast. It was misery.[8]

That Time I Married a Stranger

The story of how I married a stranger deserves a warning label. Getting married to Mr. Ireland was one in a string of impulsive decisions that defined my twenties. And, frankly, I don't think impulsive decision-making is all that unique for twenty-somethings in general. For me, nearly all my impulse decisions back then were fear-driven. I didn't realize it at the time, but now I know that I was deeply afraid of being left out or left behind. What made it worse was that my fear was exacerbated by my near-constant assessment of, and comparison to, everyone else.

So, here's the story of how I married a stranger.

The man that I married when I was twenty-four found himself in the eye of the Heidi-cane (that's a Heidi-Hurricane, for those of you that don't know). I know I couldn't have been easy to live with. But I never meant for our romance to crash and burn in the way it did and I certainly didn't intend to cause him harm. I am committed to sharing my story about him, me, and our marriage here because I believe that it might be helpful to you in some way.

---

[8] I didn't realize it, but my alcoholism and my relationship patterns with men were kicking my ass.

Ciara and Colin

I have one of the dearest, most patient, and wonderful friends on the planet and her name is Ciara. Ciara and I met in the fall of 1998 as we were rushing Delta Zeta and it was magic. She was the Paris to my Nicole, she was the good cop to my bad cop, she was the yin to my yang. Ciara was driven and focused. A ballerina and track star. She was going to be a doctor. She had decided that long ago. While, I changed my major so many times that, eventually, I just asked an advisor to cobble my credits together in a way that would give me a degree, any degree.

Ciara was ferociously committed to her dream. There were times that she took 18 credits of advanced coursework (because pre-med, duh), worked as a server at TGIFridays (it was the late nineties and she made bank at that place, Ok?) and worked a second job as an EMT. She would claim that a 48-hour shift as an EMT gave her plenty of time to sleep. But she was working in downtown Pittsburgh. It couldn't have been possible. At the time, her mother was battling breast cancer, and Ciara made sure to run the Susan G. Komen Race for the Cure each year. Even among that kind of emotional chaos, she was focused. She did all of these things, and she did it all without Adderall. She has the kind of character and drive that is the stuff that legends are made of.

Ciara dated and fell in love with a man named Colin. Colin is Irish. No, not like his last name has an O' or a Mc, like grew up on that small little island that floats out in the Atlantic. Their wedding was a destination affair and I was so honored to be invited to be a bridesmaid in it. Ciara was a saint for including me at all, because at this stage, as you know, my life was basically a rolling dumpster fire, perpetually fueled by alcohol, with no sign of letting up.

Getting to Ireland

Ciara asked me months in advance to be a member of the bridal party. Of course, I agreed. A trip to Ireland, a little break, was exactly what I needed to get back on track. I was still in Colorado, although I had relocated from Denver to Colorado Springs. I was working as a leasing agent for an apartment property there, and I was contracted to work six days a week for three months, after which, I would receive two weeks off. At the time it was a good fit. And, I lived by the old bullshit standby "work hard, play hard." Which meant that, as long as I showed up for work on time and hit my performance metrics, I could drink all the drinks in all the bars and sleep with all the strangers.

Right before I left for Ireland, I met a drifter-y guy, Mr. DarkCloud. You know the type. The dark, poetic, might be a writer, might be a serial killer, might just spend all day in the bar, but it's real hard to tell, kind of guy? I was so into this dude. His darkness, his unavailability was so attractive to me. Anyway, one night we were hanging out and his buddy was in town. I can't tell you that guy's name, or even really what he looked like. But the three of us went back to my place. We piled into bed and I legit thought I was going to have a threesome. But Mr. DarkCloud passed out. So, I fucked his friend. Right there. In the bed. Next to him.

The next morning, I had to go to work. I said bye to the guys, told them they could use my car to bop around for the day. I leased some apartments and came back to mine. It was about 6 p.m. There was no sign of them, and my car was gone. *DID THESE MOTHERFUCKERS STEAL MY CAR??* *What am I gonna tell my dad?* Those were seriously the first thoughts that crossed my mind. I paced back and forth in that apartment. I drank. I drank like they do in the movies; vodka straight from the bottle. I ran my hands through my hair. I sat down. I sighed. I stood back up. I paced. I contemplated, I evaluated, I *thought.* And then. A knock at the door. The other guy was back. He and Mr. DarkCloud had borrowed my car. They had gone to the airport and had gotten drunk (This was pre-9/11, so, if you were so inclined, you could go to an airport, head to a terminal, and drink at a bar.). Mr. DarkCloud had gotten so drunk at the bar that he had gotten in a fight with someone at the airport. He was in jail. Holy shit. There wasn't much left to do but keep drinking and fuck this guy again. So, I did.

But wait, aren't we talking about how I met my first husband? We are, but I need you to understand what my life was like. And why it seemed like the universe was delivering me another way to live, a different life, altogether, when I met Mr. Ireland. Why I was willing to turn a blind eye to so many red flags. With my life in near-constant disarray, it was impossible for me to see my marriage to my first husband as anything other than a long-overdue life preserver, a hose to the dumpster fire, an island of stability in a sea of chaos.

Ok. So, Ciara had asked me to be in her wedding and, naturally, I had agreed to it. I went to go get my bridesmaid's dress fit on the only day I could. A sick day. I needed a sick day because I had contracted a UTI that had turned into a kidney infection. I hadn't eaten anything in days, and I was feverish and sweaty. But there I was at David's Bridal, telling the seamstress to go ahead and take the dress in. If only I could have done something different that day! Maybe gone to Jamba Juice for a smoothie, and then bopped over to the mall to open a Victoria's Secret Credit card so that I could get 10% off those cutie underpants. How could I have known that asking that seamstress to remove two inches of fabric from that lavender satin bridesmaid gown with the sweetheart neckline and the white ribbon belt would alter the course of my life? Well, obviously, I couldn't have.

> With my life in near-constant disarray, it was impossible for me to see my marriage to my first husband as anything other than a long-overdue life preserver, a hose to the dumpster fire, an island of stability in a sea of chaos.

Arriving in Ireland

Two weeks later, I arrived in Ireland for the wedding. The wedding was on a Sunday. On Saturday, Colin's mother, Maggie, suggested that we all try on our wedding dresses, to be sure that everyone was all set. I remember that all the members of the bridal party squished into the front room of Maggie's home. And we were giddy with excitement; about being in Ireland, the wedding, and accents, and drinks, and boys. All of the gals zipped up their dresses. I turned to Heather, "will you zip me up"? I was doing that thing, you know, where the dress is on, the back is unzipped and you're pressing it to your body against your boobs. She pulled on the zip. And then about half way up, she said, "I can't."

"You what?!?" Panic. I had gained back the weight that I had lost when I was sick with the kidney infection. "Oh shit. This dress isn't going to zip, and it doesn't fucking fit."

We spilled out into the kitchen where Maggie had amassed a gathering of her own and my conundrum became clear to everyone. I assured them; we can just go have this tailored. On a rush. No big deal, I'll totally pay for it. But they were quick to inform me that this was Ireland, not the US. There wouldn't be any tailors open today and, certainly, no one that would do this for me by noon tomorrow.

How could I have known that asking that seamstress to remove 2 inches of fabric from that lavender satin bridesmaid gown with the sweetheart neckline and the white ribbon belt would alter the course of my life? Well, obviously, I couldn't have.

Suddenly, the groomsmen started pouring in. Oh my god, the embarrassment. One of the groomsmen, Mr. Ireland, had picked me up at the airport the day before. I hadn't paid much attention to him then; I had been recovering from a hangover and the long flight.[9]

But on this day, I noticed him. And he noticed me. And he offered to drive me down to town to try to find a tailor or seamstress who could help. So, we spent the whole afternoon looking for anyone to help me with that damn lavender satin dress, to no avail. Eventually, I think someone's mother or aunt or sister found a way to get me in that damn dress. The lavender satin was pulled so tight across my torso that a very

[9] My connecting flight had been cancelled due to a mechanical issue. The airline had put us up for the night in a hotel. While waiting to get our rooms, I had been flirting with another passenger on the flight. Once we had our room numbers, I invited this complete stranger to my room to help me "kill the mini bar." He obliged and the rest is history. Needless to say, I arrived in Ireland with a hangover and in a pretty deep shame spiral.

clear outline of my belly button is visible in every single photo I was in. I was mortified.

But I was hooked on this guy.

The groomsmen had planned a road-trip for the newlyweds and their American friends. After the wedding, we were sitting around a firepit in Colin's driveway, and Mr. Ireland turned to me and asked if I was planning to join them. Why no, I was not. Thank you very much. I had very important work I had to get back to.

But wait? Should I? "Of course, you should!" he said, "This is a once in a lifetime opportunity!"

I was scheduled to fly out back to the states the next morning. But I told myself, isn't this the stuff of life? Isn't this what it's supposed to be like to be 23? Yes, yes, it is. I called the airline and I cancelled my flight (paying through the nose to reschedule it later the next week). I called my boss and left her a voicemail; "Hello Ms. Boss. So so so so sorry, I know I was scheduled at work, but the opportunity of a lifetime just presented itself and I'm not sure I can pass it up. Good luck getting a hold of me while I'm over here bopping around! See you when I'm back."

Check, check, double check. I was set. But I hadn't planned on staying this long, I didn't have any money. I told Mr. Ireland that I was worried about that, he said "I'm loaded, I'm rich. Don't worry." And I believed him. He had been, kind of, my knight in shining armor throughout the dress debacle, so why wouldn't I trust him with this? And (honestly, I wish I hadn't been this shallow then, but I was), it was like, *oh, you've got money. That's cool. Your money will just become my money and then we can just do whatever I want with it, K?*

Mr. Ireland did have a great job, with a stable income. But he was not rich. And what really matters is that we were polar opposites when it came to finances. I like to think of myself as fiscally dangerous. Like, every time I buy something, I wish that song "Shake ya Ass" by Mystikal would come on in the background. If I could, I would embed that tune in this book, I would. Just like a birthday card that opens, and a tune comes on, it would be like you turn to this page and that song would just start. Mr. Ireland was far more conservative and reserved with the way he spent his money. I got my very first exposure to that alternative mindset (fiscal responsibility? Fiscal frugality?) on this road trip with him.

We had been on the road for four hours. Everyone was hungover from the night before. Mr. Ireland had asked me to sit all the way in the back with him and offered me his chest and lap to curl up on. And I was delighted by this. We pulled over to a gas station.

"Hey Mr. Ireland, can I borrow 5 euro to grab a Diet Coke?"

"No way, that stuff is full of chemicals and other garbage. Nope." He wasn't joking. He was dead-ass serious. I was stunned.

And that old narrative started up again, that narrative from the sixth grade; how could I have been so dumb? How could I have been so stupid; to think that a whirlwind love and romance was meant for me. Hadn't I learned my lesson by now; whirlwind love and romance was for beautiful people, not me. How could I have even dared to believe it?

My cheeks turned red, and I held back tears. I walked to the other side of the car. What the fuck. What the actual fuck am I going to do now? Now I'm stuck here for another week with this A-hole who won't even give me money for a Diet Coke. So, I did what I had always done. I focused on the money side of this equation rather than the bait and switch.

> How could I have been so stupid; to think that a whirlwind love and romance was meant for me. Hadn't I learned my lesson by now? Whirlwind love and romance was for beautiful people, not me.

At the next stop, I called my dad and pleaded with him to send me $1000.00. It could be a birthday gift, and early Christmas gift, anything. I swore I'd never do anything like this again. He wired the money. And I spent the rest of the trip trying to forget and explain away what had happened at that very first stop. Ignoring every flag of every color that popped up. Willfully constructing my "fairy-tale" romance.

At 23, I didn't think it would matter to have a different financial paradigm than my partner. Turns out, it does. But two partners with different financial paradigms can work through it together if they are both willing to surface and have some uncomfortable conversation about it. But Mr. Ireland and I never could really get to those difficult discussions. Both of us were much more likely to just push our feelings down than to come forward and tell the other how we were feeling.

And that became the biggest problem with our courtship. Both of us were completely emotionally unavailable. Initially, I thought the problem was that he was geographically unavailable, because he lived in Ireland and I lived in Denver. But when he received a transfer, and I moved to Portland, OR, to live with him (we'd only been dating long-distance for about six months), I realized how emotionally unavailable he was. And it was only in sobriety, with the clarity of hindsight and a lot of therapy, that I discovered that I was emotionally unavailable to him as well.

Marrying Mr. Ireland

About a week after Mr. Ireland moved to Portland, he asked me to join him. It was January in Denver. I had been ignoring the blocked toilet in my apartment for weeks (you'd be amazed what you can ignore when there is a second bathroom and you're willing to just keep the lid down), all my stuff fit in my car, and you guys- this man asked me to move in with him! No one that I had dated had ever done that before. I made the move. I arrived at his apartment and worked on making all of his things mine.

A month later, we were doing, I guess, what normal couples do. We were hanging out at our apartment; we had a grabbed a couple of six-packs and we were watching the Super Bowl. Mr. Ireland, was on my right and he turned to me, pushed my shoulder a little bit - and said, "Hey, wanna get married?" Ahh, it's what every girl dreams of, isn't it? That her slightly buzzed boyfriend will take time during the commercial break of a football game to casually ask her to spend the rest of her life with him.

"Yes, absolutely." I didn't give it much thought, honestly. All my friends were all doing this, and I wasn't going to be left behind. Plus, Mr. Ireland was pretty-Ok.

One catch, he said, no one could know.

> ... it's what every girl dreams of, isn't it? That her slightly buzzed boyfriend will take time during the commercial break of a football game to casually ask her to spend the rest of her life with him.

We kept it quiet. Well, quietish, I'm not great at keeping secrets.

Eventually, I told both my parents. And in May of that year, they joined us at the Courthouse, where Mr. Ireland and I said "I do" in front of a Justice of the Peace. He in a shirt and tie, me in a white suit from Banana Republic. As we walked out of the court-house, my father congratulated me, "Hey H! You're leaving a courthouse - and you're not in handcuffs!"

In June, we moved to Ireland. We moved in with Mr. Ireland's parents. They were as Irish-Catholic as I had ever met and did not know that we were married. To say they were incredibly tolerant and kind to me is an understatement. I had never considered myself a liar or dishonest. And yet, before I could really think about it, I was in a foreign country and living a tremendous lie; I was married and not a single person in this country knew. I did what I could to just try to fit in. I tried to make Mr. Ireland's friends become my friends, I drove a Fiat, I smoked Benson & Hedges, and I drank Heineken on ice.

I worked as a head-hunter. I made hundreds of cold calls each day to pitch our firm's recruitment services. Normally, I wouldn't have stood a chance at this. But working in sales in Ireland, my American accent and my perseverance were my best assets. Secretaries who were quick to cut off my colleagues assumed that I was calling from their US branch. Often, I found myself quickly connected right to the decision maker… who was inevitably deeply disappointed to find themselves talking to me. But working gave me a sense of purpose and identity, and so when I had good days at work, it was glorious. But, when I had bad days at work, it was awful.

Mr. Ireland worked nights and I struggled. I struggled to be quiet while he slept in our little townhouse. I struggled to make a home for us. I struggled to cook, and when I did cook, it was very bad. There was a lasagna incident once that ended with me throwing away every shred of evidence that I had cooked. I scraped the disgusting, burnt lasagna out of the pan and into the trash. Then I looked at the Pyrex baking dish and determined it would never be the same and that it was evidence of my failure. I wrapped it in paper towels and threw it away. Then I looked at the trash - more evidence. So took the trash and I put it in a big, black, heavy duty garbage bag. I took the bag outside to the bin. Then, I panicked - what if someone looked in the bin and saw how full it was? They would know!! They would know I had failed at something. So, I rolled the bin all the way down to the curb.

It felt like everything I did was wrong, and I was lonely. Everyone who lived where we lived had known each other for generations. I was an outsider, an afterthought, a nothing. There was so much to adjust to. And I found it terribly difficult.

Eventually, we moved back to the States. I thought that would fix everything. But, even back home, it was more of the same. I just never got the feeling that I was enough or that our marriage was enough. I always felt like I was in quicksand, and that the more I struggled and fought, the farther down I sank. And eventually, it felt like my marriage was drowning me, suffocating me, extinguishing me.

Leaving Mr. Ireland

With Mr. Ireland, I walked on eggshells from the very beginning. When things were uncomfortable, they were very uncomfortable. And, I did everything I could to try to "fix" it, except to talk about it, of course. I spent years hiding my feelings and our marriage became emptier and I got lonelier. My marriage to Mr. Ireland was deeply rooted in fear. I was always afraid that Mr. Ireland would leave me. I was afraid that I would say or do something that couldn't be undone. Eventually, I was paralyzed by fear because I thought everything I said and did was wrong. And the anxiety around that fear was absolutely crushing.

This fear made me completely unavailable to him; because it really meant that I didn't trust the resiliency of our relationship. I didn't trust that it could sustain a few bumps in the road, and I wasn't willing to test it. I didn't trust that Mr. Ireland could love my full, true self, so I was always managing my emotions in order to manage his response to them. Always modifying how I expressed myself so as to avoid causing him any discomfort. I was never able to just be me. I wasn't even willing to try it. Mr. Ireland wasn't married to Heidi. He was married to a watered-down version of her, a Heidi-Lite.

Mr. Ireland had a part too, some of his behaviors exacerbated these fears of mine. For example, when Mr. Ireland got mad at me about something (be it getting in the way in the bathroom, to forgetting to make a credit card payment on time, to my $4/day latte habit) he would stuff all of his feelings down and then he would freeze me out. There were periods of time where he would a week without saying a single word to me.

> I didn't trust that Mr. Ireland could love my full, true self, so I was always managing my emotions in order to manage his response to them. Always modifying how I expressed myself so as to avoid causing him any discomfort.

Ironically, when times were really bad with us and we would fight (before the freeze out that inevitably followed) Mr. Ireland would say, "You know, Heidi, you can lie to them. You can lie to me. But you can't lie to yourself." This was infuriating to hear during a fight. It was so patronizing and paternalistic. But in the end, I realized it was true. And it had been in front of my face the whole time. My biggest regret around the time I spent with Mr. Ireland, is that it was uncomfortable from the beginning and yet, I spent years trying to convince myself that if only I was better, if only I behaved better, was less forgetful, had better or different feelings, then we would be able to connect and we would find joy in one another. And the truth is, I finally couldn't really lie to myself anymore; as much as Mr. Ireland and I might have wanted to find joy in one another, we never really could.

I decided to leave Mr. Ireland. A girlfriend of mine said I could stay at her place for a couple of days. I asked another girlfriend if I could rent a room from her, she agreed. I came home from school one evening[10] and I told Mr. Ireland that we needed to talk.

"Uh, I'm watching Grey's Anatomy," he said.

I grabbed the remote and muted the show. I told him I had packed a bag, I was leaving, and I was staying with a friend for the night. I told him that while he was at work the next day, I would come back for the rest of my things.

He would change! He argued. I owed him a chance to change.

In the end, I decided that the kind of changes that both of us needed to make couldn't be made over the course of a couple of months. We needed years. If we each took some time and did some work and came back to one another, that would be fine. But I couldn't risk staying with him and letting anymore of myself get lost in the eggshells. I knew that if I didn't leave that day, I wouldn't ever be able to leave. I felt that. Like, in my soul. It was me or our marriage. And I chose me.

Choosing me and leaving Mr. Ireland was devastating. And while I was in the, *should I stay? or should I go?* phase, I was more uncomfortable than I have ever been in my whole life. But once I had made the best choice for me, the anxiety largely evaporated. I saw a therapist on my own, I did group therapy, I focused on my doctoral work, I drank (more on that in the next chapter). I heard two bits of advice during this time period that have always stuck with me. One was from my therapist at the time, Mr. Therapist, the other from a nurse who was answering calls on a crisis line.

---

[10] I had been pursuing a Ph.D. in Political Science/Public Affairs and Policy at Portland State University.

When I left Mr. Ireland, my mom (of all people), suggested that I commit to 30 days of no contact with him. What?!? I couldn't believe the audacity of this suggestion. How dare she suggest that I block him on Facebook, that I block his emails to me, that I block or delete his phone number? Didn't she know that I needed to argue with him, that we had shit to square away, that he deserved to know how I felt about him? I don't know how or why, but even though I didn't want to, I followed most of this advice. I did block him on Facebook (Instagram wasn't a thing, or I would have blocked him there too). I did block his phone number. I didn't block his email; my rationalization being that I needed some way to contact him regarding divorce proceedings and that this was the least intrusive.

So, I was doing this 30-days-no-contact-thing and I was complaining to Mr. Therapist that I felt like I was getting gypped. I deserved closure. I deserved to know how Mr. Ireland was feeling, how miserable he was, how much he missed me and, obviously, how letting me go and treating me badly had become his life's biggest regret. Also, I deserved to be able to tell him how I felt, how this had been hard for me too, that I had regrets, and to reassure him that I wasn't the bitch that he surely thought I was. Mr. Therapist took a deep breath. He leaned forward and put his elbows on his knees, he pressed the tips of his fingers together and placed the tops of his middle fingers just below his chin. He said to me, "Heidi, we don't always get closure." And you know what? He's right. I'd like to think that I'm entitled to everything being tidied up into a nice, neat, little box with a bow. And it doesn't always go that way. In fact, sometimes, it's just enough that we get to set the boundary or leave the toxic relationship.

A few months later, the wheels were coming off. In an attempt to find a way into a rehab facility, I made a call to a crisis line. The on-call nurse offered me a spot in an outpatient program, but I refused. I remember talking with the

> I deserved closure. I deserved to know how Mr. Ireland was feeling, how miserable he was, how much he missed me and, obviously, how letting me go and treating me badly had become his life's biggest regret.

nurse on the phone and telling her that I couldn't go because then Mr. Ireland would be right. About what? When we had been married, occasionally, he would turn to me, totally out of the blue, and say, "God, where would you even be without me? What would you even do? You know, you'd probably end up back in Iowa." I told her, surrendering in this fight I was having with alcohol would make him right. And she said, "Maybe it makes him right maybe it doesn't, but is it really worth destroying your life over?" I didn't know. Was it? It felt like it might be. I really didn't want him to be right. I didn't take that opportunity to get sober, but it brought me closer to the opportunity that I did take. And as I approached it, I thought about what that nurse said over and over again. And the more I thought about it, the shorter the sentence got. Until, eventually, it was just, "Is it really worth destroying your life over?" And finally, one day, it wasn't.

4

THANK GOD FOR GOOGLE MAPS

What made me an alcoholic? What does alcoholism look like? For me, it wasn't like I just started drinking one day and couldn't stop. It started long before that with what I believe is an allergy of the body and a disease of the mind. I have a magic magnifying mind which means I can make a mountain out of a molehill of just about anything. I've come to consider it just an extreme form of self-centeredness. Combine the extreme self-centeredness with a bodily allergy to alcohol, and suddenly, everyone is looking at me. Everyone is judging me. No one likes me. No one is like me. Suddenly, I find myself carrying on an argument from weeks ago for hours while I drink a beer in the shower as I get ready. And the kicker is that once I put that first drink in my system, my body demands more.

I grew up in an alcoholic household. While I was growing up, both of my parents drank. And man did they party. They threw epic parties. They had a polka party one year, where they turned our garage into a polka hall and they hired a polka band, and there were two kegs, and people spilled out of our garage, down the driveway, and into the street. And, as a shy young kid, I watched my parents throw these epic ragers, and I wanted to be like them. I remember thinking, *I want that. I want that, for sure.*

I had my first drink at fifteen. I was running around with a little nerdy group of kids. One of the boys in our little pack could grow a beard and so, one night, he bought us a six-pack of Bud Ice. Three of us were excited to drink and so we split the six-pack three ways. I had two beers. I blacked out. I loved it. What I really loved was who I became when I drank. I loved that during the day I was this straight-A, goody two shoes student, but that when I had a drink, I was funny. And I fit in. And, in the beginning, people wanted me around. It was magic and it felt amazing. And once we got started, I couldn't understand why we would ever stop.

In my late teens and early twenties, I started to do some journaling. I still have these journals and I call them my "death journals." I would go out and drink, then come home and start writing. I would start out writing in pen and the words flew across the page. But, inevitably, the pen would run out of ink. So I would grab a lip liner and, eventually, I would reach the edge of the page, but then, instead of just going to the next line, I would just turn the journal 90 degrees and write down the margin, trailing off, with some drunken stream of consciousness thought. Every once in a while, I have a look at those journals. They're sad. My thoughts were consumed with, *What's wrong with me? I'm so sorry. I don't know what's wrong with me. I can't fix this. I don't know how to fix this.* It's just, like, page after page of the same thing.

If my death journals taught me anything it was that, subconsciously, I knew that alcohol wasn't working for me the way that it had worked when I took that first drink. And I was pissed. At the beginning of the night, alcohol would make me feel like I belonged; like I was a part of the party. But, the end of the night was a different story. By the end of a night of drinking, I would find myself at some house party with a bunch of people at three in the morning. And I would look around and see that everyone was either passed out or making out, but I'd still be up, by myself, with a bottle of vodka. Thinking, *well, those guys are losers. I can't believe they're missing this. There's still vodka left in this bottle.* Because alcohol was all I could think about. It was the center of my universe. And it was terribly isolating, to end up alone, with a bottle, night after night after night.

And of course, all this time, my life was in session. When I was eighteen, my mom took a drug overdose that kills almost two-thirds of the people who take it. As a result, she ended up in treatment and got sober, and today she has twenty-one years of sobriety, which is amazing. She and my dad got divorced. And I watched my father drink himself to death. His alcoholism was different than mine. He was a maintenance drinker, and he became chained to the bottle. Cocktail hour started at 4:00 at our house when I was growing up. And what used to be cocktails at 4:00 turned into a cocktail at 4:00, then one at 6:00, one at 8:00, 10:00, midnight, and then up at 2:00 a.m., 4:00 a.m., 6:00 a.m. When he died, he had been sitting at our kitchen table, drinking and smoking for years—a tumbler full of vodka on the rocks in his left hand, cigarettes in his right. When we cleaned out the house, I looked at the table and realized that he had worn away the varnish on our kitchen table in the shape of two arms. And that is a visual that I'll never forget.

My dad died when I was twenty-eight. By thirty, I had decided I didn't want to be married anymore. I wanted to live my life the way that I wanted. I wanted to drink the way I wanted. I wanted to hang

> At the beginning of the night, alcohol would make me feel like I belonged; like I was a part of the party. But, the end of the night was a different story.

out the way I wanted. So, while I did take to opportunity to choose me in that marriage, my behavior afterward was compelled by my alcoholism. As I was getting divorced, I went on one last year-long bender. And, the unpredictability of my alcoholism started to get me in trouble. In that last year, my brain would tell me, *I'm getting maximized, I'm getting all dressed up, and I'm going downtown. I'm gonna go drink some Cosmopolitans. I'm gonna meet a hot guy. We're gonna talk about art and travel. It's going to be great. It will basically be like I'm living in 'Sex and the City.'*

Okay, so here's the thing, I don't know anything about art or travel. But it doesn't really even matter because when I drink, I don't meet Mr. Art or Mr. Travel. When I drink, I make it to the corner bar on the street that I live on. I sit down at the bar. I'm not drinking Cosmos; I'm drinking vodka on ice out of a pint glass. As I'm drinking it, I end up talking to a guy that's been there all day. And, trust me, he also doesn't know anything about travel or art. But the scariest part about the whole thing is that once I start drinking, I have almost no control over what will happen to me at the end of the night. And, I just don't know where I'll go or who I'll go home with.

One night, I did make it out of my little neighborhood and to a bar downtown. And I did meet a guy. And we might have even discussed travel! I had several drinks with him at a fancy little spot called the Portland City Grill. The lounge at the Portland City Grill is complete with warm colors and dark wood, a great happy hour, and a baby grand that sits center stage with a piano man who takes requests. It always feels, like, so rich to be there. Eventually, Mr. City Grill asked me if I wanted to leave and I decided to get in the car with him. We drove to his house about 30 minutes away. We definitely did stuff there. But, at 4:00 a.m. , I remembered something: he had mentioned that his ex was going to be dropping his kiddo off at 8:00 a.m. My mind raced, *Oh my god. I do not want to be here. I do not want to be here at all. Ok. Ok. Ok. I'll call a cab.* I got my phone out, and realized, *Holy shit. I don't know where I am.* I Google Maps'ed myself. I found some cross streets.

I called a cab, "Yeah, I'm at the corner of blah, blah, blah and blah, blah, blah."

"Okay. I'll be there in a minute," the cab driver responded. Five minutes later, the cab driver called me back. He said, "I'm sorry, but the cross streets you gave me don't exist. I don't know where you're at."

I said to him, "Listen, man, I had to Google Maps myself to even give you that. I don't know where I'm at either, and I really need you to come get me."

He said to me, "Are you at a guy's house?"

"Yep."

He said, "Most people keep their mail in the kitchen. Go to the kitchen and start looking for his mail?"

"Genius!"

I kept him on the phone, ran into the kitchen, and started going through this guy's kitchen drawers. And, finally, it was as if the clouds had parted and the sun shone through, "Oh my god, I found the mail!" I whisper-shrieked into the phone. I gave the cab driver the address, and he came to get me. He didn't charge me the full price to take me home. Maybe he felt bad for me, maybe he thought I was cute. Who knows?

That was not my last experience like that. I continued to go out and to do what I wanted. I dated compulsively. I had been obsessed with OKCupid, and I had been on a date with a guy who had wanted to meet me for coffee. At the time, I thought, *Ew, okay.* I couldn't understand why we would meet for coffee when we could have met for drinks. But I went and met him anyway. We were having coffee, and I was bored. When he got up to get a second coffee I said, "Nice to meet you. See you never. I'm out of here," and I left.

I was trying all kinds of stuff to avoid getting sober, so for a while I became obsessive about working out. I felt like; a real alcoholic wouldn't be able to work out the way I was. So, every day, I was putting in work at the gym, and I kept seeing the same flyer in the bathroom stall. You know like the flyers that have the phone number tabs that you can rip off and take home? The flyer said, "Do you play racquetball? I need a racquetball partner. E-mail or call Cynthia at..."—blah, blah, blah, blah. Every once in a while, I'd look at those flyers, like "God, this poor bitch is still looking for that racquetball partner." As much as I wanted the gym and working out to be the answer to my alcoholism, it wasn't.

I said to him, "Listen, man, I had to Google Maps myself to even give you that. I don't know where I'm at either, and I really need you to come get me."

I continued to build the scaffolding of my life up and then take a match to it and burn it to the ground. I thought I was doing what I wanted. But my behavior was driven by an obsessive mind and a compulsion to drink until I blacked out. It was more or less always a train-wreck and the last night that I drank was no different. But, for some reason, on 9/10/11, I woke up, and I had a moment of clarity. "I'm done. Mercy. I give. I'm done. I can't do this."

I think that part of the reason that happened was that it became really clear to me that there were only two options for me. This disease was either going to kill me, or I was going to get sober. All I had to do was to look at my parents. I really wished that I had more options, oh my God, did I want there to be another way, but there were only the two. I decided to give sobriety a shot. I waited for three days until I walked through the doors of a twelve-step meeting. Because I just wanted to be able to get and stay sober on my own. But on my third day without a drink, I felt like I might kill someone. That was a scary feeling - not being able to make it through three days without a drink- and it was a real shock for me. I didn't know exactly what to do except I knew my mom went to twelve-step meetings. Desperate and scared, I decided I would give twelve-step recovery a try.

I was meticulous about finding the perfect twelve-step meeting. I was sure that if I went to one that was at a prestigious, local university; there would be no discussion of God. Religiosity, spirituality, these would not be requirements. The discussion of sobriety would be very logical. I found a meeting that I thought would fit these criteria and decided I would go.

The universe is funny. I hadn't showered, I was chain-smoking cigarettes, let's just say it wasn't my best look. I walked into my first twelve-step meeting, and that OKCupid, coffee-date guy was standing at the door and greeting everyone as they came in. Yeah. He recognized me and said, "Hey, how are you?" and I responded, "How am I? How do you think I am? I'm at fucking twelve-step meeting?!?!" At that stage, I couldn't think of why there'd be any other answer to that question. I was devastated, I was miserable, I was scared.

Anyway, I don't know how or why, but instead of turning around and walking right back out the door, I sat down and I listened. When the group went around introducing themselves, I couldn't bring myself to say my name and admit that I was the "A-word." But I found myself laughing with them and nodding along when they talked. I found that the message of alcoholics in recovery was resonating with me.

Even though Mr. OKCupid had been very nice to me at the door, I decided that there was no way I could go back to that meeting. I had to find a new one. I went back home, and I consulted the Portland Area Intergroup website, in order to find a new meeting, and the next night, there was a meeting at a Presbyterian church in Mount Tabor. I decided I'd give it a try.

I went to that meeting. I was four days sober and still very uncomfortable. I got there, and there were no chairs, no lights, no people, no cookies, and no coffee. And I found myself so agitated that I thought, "OMG. I'm going to kill someone over the fact that there's not a meeting here WHEN THERE IS SUPPOSED TO BE A MEETING HERE!!" I was pacing back and forth, I was huffing and puffing, folding my arms and stomping my feet, having a toddler-style meltdown in the basement of this church.

A woman walked by, she said, "Do you need a meeting?"

"Yeah, yeah, I do. I fucking need a meeting."

And she said, "Well, there's a CODA meeting upstairs." I didn't know that CODA stands for Codependents Anonymous. I was adamant about not belonging there, although I very certainly could have used a dose of Codependents Anonymous. But I was desperate and crazy, so I went upstairs with that woman and I sat down among a group of about ten people who were talking about codependency and its attendant unmanageability.

The previous day, I could not identify as an alcoholic. At this meeting, I was immediately like, "I'm Heidi. I'm an alcoholic. I am not like you people. You know, alcoholics are the apex predators of the addiction world. We are the great white sharks of addiction. Codependents Anonymous - I don't understand it - you guys are like bottom feeders."

The egotistical lunacy of the words that came out of my mouth astounds me to this day. The people in that meeting showed me such kindness and grace that day. They hugged me after the meeting. They asked if I would be Ok. They didn't care

> You know, alcoholics are the apex predators of the addiction world. We are the great white sharks of addiction.

that I was clearly out of my mind. After the meeting, a young man approached me. He didn't try to give me his number. He didn't try to pick me up. He said to me, "I'm in another twelve-step program, and you sound like you really need to talk. Let's go for a walk around the block."[11]

I did and I went with him. We walked around the block, and he saved my life that night. He said, "Do you think you can just go home and go to bed sober tonight?" I nodded. And then he said, "Just keep coming back. Just keep trying something different," and I said, "Ok."

So, the next night, I needed to find another new meeting. I was frustrated and I remember thinking, "Oh, my god, when am I going to find a meeting that I can just keep going to?" It was a Friday night and I hadn't spent very many Friday nights sober. I had a closetful of cute clothes. I decided, "I'm going to get maximized and go to a meeting."

I put on a mini skirt and some high heels, and I went to a meeting that I'd found called Scully's. Scully's has a history as one of the longest-running twelve-step meetings in the Pacific Northwest. It's an amazing place and there are a lot of really hard case alcoholics who get sober there. I had arrived on this particular Friday night all dressed up to go out and I had a really hard time finding any similarities between me and the other people there. When the meeting ended, I was on my way out and I thought, "I'm out of here. This is bullshit. I don't need this," and another guy caught up with me just outside the door. He wasn't trying to pick me up. He said, "You know, you look like you are having a hard time fitting in here," and I

---

[11] In light of predatory behavior in some rooms of 12-step recovery, I think it's important to clarify that this young man was only concerned about my ability to stay sober for the evening.

agreed, I was. And then he suggested that the Alano Club in Portland might be more my speed. He wanted to know if I could stay sober that evening, I told him that I wasn't crazy about it but that I could. And he said, "Great, by the way, my name's Mr. Angel." After I wrapped up my conversation with him, I got in my car and headed home. Another day sober in the books.

The next day, I attended a meeting in the basement of the Portland Alano Club, and I finally felt like, "Oh, finally, I'm here! I get it." I breathed a sigh of relief. Because I had finally found a meeting where I could hear the message of recovery and I felt comfortable enough to go back to it. The point is, sometimes we have to just keep coming back. Sometimes it's not easy to find our way in sobriety or life. Sometimes we have to endure some discomfort in order to keep trying something different.

After I'd found my spot in the Alano Club, I put about two weeks of continuous sobriety together, and Mr. Angel showed back up. After a meeting one day he said, "Oh, hey. Have you met my friend, Cynthia?" I hadn't. "Cynthia," he said, "this is Heidi. Heidi, you should work the steps with Cynthia." It was so awkward, but I said, "Okay. Are you sponsoring me now?" and Cynthia said, "Yeah, if you want to do the work." It was a really brief interaction. She gave me her phone number, and that was that.

I had about 60 days sober, and I was meeting with my sponsor, Cynthia. We were talking about some stuff, and then all of a sudden, she looked at me and said, "This isn't part of the steps, but you're a pretty active person, do you play racquetball? I've had this flyer up for a while at my gym and I am really looking for a racquetball partner." My Cynthia, my first sponsor in this twelve- step program that was saving my life, was the person who had been looking for a racquetball partner for years at the gym that I had been going to all along.

I didn't know it, but Cynthia had been in my life, accessible to me for years before I had really needed her. Years before I met her and started to work the twelve steps with her and started to receive the gifts of sobriety through that work. I always think that I know what's going on and that I can see the big picture. But the reality is, I'm doing a double-sided puzzle that's all

"This isn't part of the steps, but you're a pretty active person, do you play racquetball? I've had this flyer up for a while at my gym and I am really looking for a racquetball partner."

black, and there are no edges. I don't have all the pieces. I don't know what's going on. If I let go and just do what I'm supposed to do here, my Higher Power brings me the thing I need. So that's pretty amazing.

I could write an entirely different book about my twelve-step experiences and I hope that I have an opportunity to do so. For now, I will say, I kept going back. I kept going back to twelve-step meetings and they saved my life. They helped me to get out of my own way and to discover my true self. It was not easy, the journey of sobriety has required more courage, patience, help, and discomfort than I ever imagined. But it has made me the woman who I am today. A woman who is an available and loving partner, who does what she says she will, and who has long-term, sustainable friendships.

5

BOUNDARIES

Now that we're friends, I am sure it will come as no shock to you that, for most of my adult life, I struggled with the ability to have sustainable romantic relationships. Each relationship I was in was a flurry of fantasy, fear, joy, and devastation. Each ride on the relationship roller coaster took a larger toll on my self-esteem and wellbeing.

The last "relationship" I was in was the one that prepared me to do this work. Let's call a spade a spade, I was screwing a guy who was in a relationship with another woman. For weeks, he and I would get together and just fuck. No movies, no dinner, not even much chit-chat. Just the pure, unadulterated (yes, I can see the irony) fantasy of walking in the door and getting down to it. Eventually, he split up with his girl, but we continued our trysts, which I affectionately thought of as highly efficient. Finally, one day he said, "I don't think I can objectify you like this. Can we go to dinner or something?" and I replied, "Well, that would be dating." He said, "But, Heidi, I can't date you. I don't want to date you." He was incredulous, disgusted, annoyed. And it was awful, because I had always assumed that, someday after the dust settled with his ex, he would want to date me.

After months of hemming and hawing about kind of wanting to get out of this but not really, I finally I walked away from him. I called a girlfriend

> I am here to tell you, you are worthy of self-love, you are worthy of the love of another human being, you are worthy of romantic love and deep intimacy. And all of it is possible

who had done some work around men and relationships and I told her I was finally ready for something different. And then, she and I quit him cold turkey. With her help, I blocked him on all my social media accounts, I replaced his name in my phone with "DO NOT CALL THIS NUMBER," and I became willing to do some deep soul-searching about the woman that I had become. I did the soul-searching, I did the writing, I took some suggestions, I talked to other women, I freakin' prayed, I meditated, and eventually something miraculous happened. I found myself in a position of neutrality around this guy. Once I was completely indifferent to him, it was easy as "boy, bye" to delete his contact info from my phone.

Maybe you're tired of being someone's rebound, or sick of being a "friend with benefits?" Maybe you struggle to honor your authenticity as soon as you are aware of an admirers' gaze? Maybe you can identify with some of my experiences, or maybe you're ready to try something new? Until I did the work that I've outlined here, I absolutely could not understand how other people were sustaining LTRs. I was certain that they were for other people but not for me. I am here to tell you, you are worthy of self-love, you are worthy of the love of another human being, you are worthy of romantic love and deep intimacy. And all of it is possible.

So, let's get down to it. Let's do this work together. I can't guarantee that the universe will deliver you a relationship the minute that you're done. But, I can guarantee that, when you're finished, you will know more about yourself, your patterns of behavior, and the various manifestations of the most intense emotions in your life (like fear and anger) in your relationship behavior. The exercises that I've outlined in the next 8 chapters, helped me find and honor my capital -T TRUTH. And I know they will do the same for you.

I did not do this work on my own. A dear friend of mine, Ms. Warrior Spirit, helped me. When I had questions and frustrations, I called her, texted her, and emailed her. I'd love to help anyone who is willing to do this work, so if you need an accountability partner, call me. If you don't call me, I would strongly encourage you to find someone you trust to talk to about this. I will always cheerlead you on to talk about your feelings, about the writing you're doing, and about the growth you're experiencing.

Generally, this kind of soul-searching is best done outside of relationships/flirtation/attention from people you find attractive. So, if you are a heterosexual woman, this work requires that you limit your one-on-one communication with heterosexual men. While I was doing these exercises and all this writing I did not call, text, or DM men on any of the socials. And I only hung out with men in mixed company, meaning that there were other women present when I was spending time with men.

This required me to set some boundaries with the men in my life. First, I had to reach out to a number of men that had been part of my crew. I had to tell them that I was taking some time to do some work on men and relationships. That I needed some space from them to do that. This about that: I absolutely did not want to say those words and yet I found myself willing to say them. And, overwhelmingly, this kind of honesty was met with respect and awe. With men in my life generally wishing me the best of luck and asking me to get in touch when the time was right.

Next, I had to learn to set some boundaries with men who were barking up my tree (you know, guys that I was casually seeing, guys that I was stringing along in case I wanted to be seeing them, etc). When those men reached out to me, I politely informed them that some things had changed for me. I was doing some work on men and relationships and so I wasn't available. I wasn't entirely willing to let some of these guys go, and so I told them that I would be back in touch when I was finished. Hey, progress not perfection, right? Though not ideal, this bought

> This boundary-setting exercise alone, helped me to begin to trust the universe. For my own sanity, I had to believe that anyone who was supposed to in my life would be around when this work was done.

me some time and space to do this work. And, in that time and space, I grew and changed into a woman who wasn't interested in those guys anymore. So, I didn't get back to them. And that was A-Ok. This boundary-setting exercise, alone helped me to begin to trust the universe. For my own sanity, I had to believe that anyone who was supposed to in my life would be around when this work was done.

By taking this step, without even having done much writing, I had already learned a couple of things. First, my life is infinitely easier when I am honest. Generally, communicating the simplest form of the truth is the best way to do this. For me, Ego—in the form of complexity and over-explaining—is the enemy of simple truth. Ego wanted me to tell those guys, "oh well, you know it's just this thing and it's not a big deal and, yeah, I'm not all-in on it, so I can probably manage to talk to you on the side while I do it." Ego wanted to be in control. Ego wanted me to over-explain to these guys what I was doing, so that I could make sure that they understood. And in turn, Ego and I would be able to control how those guys thought about me. And at this beginning stage, controlling how or what people thought about me was pretty high on my list of priorities.

I heard this saying and I love it—you can either save your ass or you can save your face, but you can't save both. What it means is if I really want to have an authentic and badass life, I have to show up for it and tell people what's really going on for me. I have to save my ass. No more, "I'm fine, everything's great." No more using my socials to imply that my life is perfect. That is saving face. Saving your ass requires that you find at least one person you can be completely fucking honest with. And calling them when your ass is on fire. It means finding some willingness to do something that you don't want to do, or that's not easy to do, or that doesn't save face, in order to have an authentic life. Saving your ass requires setting your ego aside. This isn't easy because ego cares about what other people think, and so it always wants you to save your face instead of your ass. For this work, setting ego aside looked like being honest with people about what I was doing and why I was doing it. And really, it came down to this; I was sick and tired of harming myself with relationships, and I was finally ready to do something different. Even if that included setting my Ego aside.

Second, my perspective around setting boundaries was completely altered by this work. Maybe I'm a sucker, maybe I didn't have great relationships modeled for me, maybe I watched too many rom-coms. But all my life, I assumed that if I set a boundary with a person and they actually respected it, it meant they didn't love me. And vice versa, that if I set a boundary with a person and they trampled all over it (they called and texted when I asked them to give me space, they showed up at my work when I asked them not to, etc.) it meant they *did* love me.

I want to talk about both sides of this coin a little more. Pop culture and movies craft a convincing narrative around the trampling of boundaries. In, like basically every rom-com ever made, the female protagonist tells her suitor *I'm not that interested,* or *I'm busy.* Instead of respecting the boundary that she's set, our plucky suitor generally perseveres. If he respected her initial boundary the movie would take an entirely different direction. Perhaps one in which we watch our badass female protagonist launch her homemade soap business, or we follow her on a trip around the world, or we cheer her on as she crosses the finish line of her first triathlon.

> You can either save your ass or you can save your face, but you can't save both.

But this isn't that movie. Instead, he just keeps showing up. He shows up with flowers at her work, he comes through for her in a pinch, he wins over her family (undermining her own judgment of his character), and eventually, he wins her over too. Listen, I'm all about pop culture and the modern rom-com, I am, and I don't want to take it too seriously. I just want to acknowledge that growing up watching that stuff shaped my perspective as a young woman on what having good boundaries looked like.

Just before I got sober, I met a guy: Mr. Bike Messenger. A few weeks into sobriety, I realized that I had to tell Mr. Bike Messenger that I couldn't see him anymore. I needed a 30-Day Mr. Bike Messenger Detox. This did not go over well with Mr. Bike Messenger. He called and texted non-stop. And you

But this isn't that movie. Instead, he just keeps showing up. He shows up with flowers at her work, he comes through for her in a pinch, he wins over her family (undermining her own judgment of his character), and eventually, he wins her over too.

know, I couldn't resist, so I would call him back. There would be explanations and tears along with lots of promises. There were insane discussions about Mr. Bike Messenger moving to Portland to get sober too. It was a complete disaster. It was like, every time I started to feel settled about what I had decided for myself, I would pick up the phone and there would be a message from him, and I would - I guess - rip the band-aid off and start to bleed again. I never gave myself enough distance from him to let the wound scab over.

But the truth is, my ego loved the chaos and drama of having a guy's attention. My ego loved it so much that even when I wasn't interested in him, I still found his attention intoxicating. Even when it was dangerous to my early sobriety, I didn't care. I needed this attention and validation from Mr. Bike Messenger. I wish that I could say that Mr. Bike Messenger was the only man with whom I experienced this, but he's not. Eventually, I got to a place where my friend Pat had to remind me that "people are not playthings." I'm not proud of that. But, as a consequence of all my baggage, and all the stuff I eventually had to grow through, I found male attention so alluring that she had to remind me that it's not cool to play with someone's heart.

On the flip side, there were plenty of times that I set boundaries with men and they respected them as a grown-ass man should. Until I did some deep soul searching, I nearly always interpreted this respected boundary as a sign that there was something wrong with me. I can guarantee you that there were men I set boundaries with who definitely weren't interested. But I think there were probably also men who were into me but heard me say I wasn't into them and turned their attention elsewhere. This almost always left me in a tailspin. "I broke up with Mr. Sigma Chi three days ago, when is he gonna show up and wait outside my class to talk to me? Where are my dozens of text messages? When will he put on a song and dance with the entire fraternity to win over my sorority sisters and, by extension, me?" And then that old voice, little sixth grade Heidi would pop up and say "What. Is. WRONG WITH YOU? How could you have been so stupid to throw that away? What the actual fuck is wrong with you, twenty-year-old Heidi?! Why would you tell someone who's interested in us that we're *not* interested in him?!?"

The tailspin of a respected boundary was the manifestation of a scarcity mindset. That there was not enough love for me. That I should just settle for what was right in front of me. That it was ridiculous to ask for more. That more was for other people and not for me. I was constantly afraid that I was making a mistake by honoring my truth and ending something that wasn't working. That I would miss out on some grand romantic adventure. A fear that I felt was confirmed when I ended something with someone who respected my boundary and moved on.

I had a lot of growing up to do before I would understand that a respected boundary was a sign of maturity. A person who respects a boundary also understands availability. Part of that growing up began here. Because when I told men that I would be unavailable for the time it took to do this, I was completely shocked when they left me alone and respected my boundary. It totally blew my wig back; I was mind-blown that these men, my friends, and acquaintances, were respecting my boundaries and that this was a sign of friendship. Woah.

So, take this boundary setting seriously. The work that you're about to do deserves your full attention. If you want to learn some real shit about your patterns and behaviors, you can't afford to be distracted.

> I had a lot of growing up to do before I would understand that a respected boundary was a sign of maturity. A person who respects a boundary also understands availability.

Yes, time will pass. Yes, this might throw off your five-year plan (depending on how long it takes, I can tell you it took me eleven months). But, anything worth doing is worth doing well. Give this one hundred percent. It doesn't have to be perfect, but it does require your attention, focus, and that you set and maintain your boundaries.

6

THE LIST

The muffled scream is my calling card. When I'm stressed out, I still either scream into a scarf or into the crook of my elbow. Even Mr. Husband, who I didn't meet until almost nine months after I was done, knows the scream and its origins. You don't choose the scream; the scream chooses you.

Ok, I'm not going to lie, this part is tough. When I did this, I wore a super-cozy infinity scarf and I screamed into it every single time I did more writing.

> The muffled scream is my calling card. You don't choose the scream, the scream chooses you.

So, what kind of work could possibly drive someone to develop a muffled-scarf-scream-habit? THE LIST. That's what. Remember, the first part of this journey requires examining old behaviors and patterns. It will be challenging, and I am giving you permission to scream, to stomp your feet, to flail around, to basically have whatever kind of temper tantrum you need to, over this.

As long as you keep moving forward.[12]

Here's what I want you to do: Make a list of all the relationships, flings, one-night stands, any person with whom you have ever had a sexual, romantic, or deeply emotional relationship. For example; maybe it was a super-charged emotional flirtation that never moved into a physical phase, but you got something out of it. That one goes on the list.

Be as thorough as you can. One word of caution: don't trip about, *does this guy count,* or *does this relationship count.* If you think it's worth writing about, count it. If you truly think there is nothing there, don't count it. But be true to yourself; don't exclude someone just because you don't feel like looking at it. If you do, you may miss some important information about yourself.

I have provided journal pages for this work at the end of this book. Use them. They provide a great template for the questions that you'll need to ask yourself and the dimensions of the relationship that you'll need to assess. Here is the information I'm asking you to record about each and every one of these physical, emotional, and romantic relationships.

(1) The name of the person with whom you were involved.

(2) Your age at the time the relationship started.

(3) Summary of relationship/Highlights/Lowlights.

(4) How did it make me feel? In what ways did this relationship affect me?

(5) Is this relationship a part of, or reflective of, a larger pattern?

(6) What was my part in the drama/chaos (if any) in this relationship?[13]

Answer all the questions by filling in all the columns for each relationship on your list. It does not matter how you fill in the matrix. Some people like

---

[12] If you have ever done a fourth step in a twelve-step recovery program, this will look very familiar! I've included it here because I believe it is truly one of the best tools available for self-examination.

[13] It is most definitely not my job to tell you what your part is or isn't in these chaotic patterns. But I'd like to add a quick note about assessing your part: if you suffered a trauma of some kind, i.e. sexual abuse, neglect, molestation, etc., you do not have a part in that. As a grown person, you do have the opportunity to find a way to heal from that; my suggestion is always discussing it with a qualified mental health professional. And doing so will undoubtedly change the way that you show up in your relationships.

to make the whole list of names and relationships first and then flush out the additional details. Some people prefer to answer each question about the relationship before moving on to the next one. I want to share a few of my personal experiences on this.

First, there were plenty of people on my list whose names I couldn't remember. So, I included them anyway. Trust me, there was more than one, "one-night stand guy from Mulligans" on my list. The point of this exercise is not that you remember, by name, every single person with whom you've had a relationship. It's to examine the *patterns* of these entanglements. So, more important than the names in the columns, are the "in what ways did this relationship affect me" and the "what was my part in this chaos" columns.

Next, use the summary column to rehash any or all of the gory details and drama of this relationship. Write as much or as little as you need to, in order to capture the essence of the experience. This whole process requires honest self-appraisal, and this section is really where the rubber begins to meet the

The point of this exercise is not that you remember, by name, every single person with whom you've had a relationship. It's to examine the *patterns* of these entanglements.

road. Be honest with this. What really happened in this relationship? Get that reality on paper, write it down, put it in black and white. Don't worry about saving face here, use this exercise to save your ass. Write it the fuck down.

As you move through the columns, begin to streamline the writing. So that when you get to the next column, the "in what way did this relationship affect you?" column, you can start to search for the simplest, honest, answer. As you evaluate the material for this column, you can say to yourself "this relationship affected my _____" and just fill in the blank in that column; i.e. *self-esteem, self-worth, emotional well-being, finances, pride, ego, relationships with my friends, mental health, security*, etc. There are seriously so many words and phrases that can go in this column and you can list as many as you need to in order to thoroughly capture the way that this relationship affected you.

For the column "what was my part in the drama/chaos of this relationship?" do your best to keep it to simple words and phrases here, too, i.e., *entitled, self-pitying, childish, attention-seeking, manipulative, controlling, jealous, afraid, angry, dishonest,* etc. It won't take long for you to see your patterns. I had started to see patterns of the way my relationships affected me before I even got to the "My Part" column. And when I got to the "My Part" column, an entirely new set of patterns emerged, and I had to get my scream scarf out again.

I got tired of writing the phrases *attention-seeking, seeking outside of self, seeking-validation, entitled, dishonest,* and *childish* in the "My Part" column by the time I got to the second relationship and I had, like, 70 more to do. **Write it the fuck down.** But, don't sell yourself short by quitting after the first few relationships when you see your first pattern. There is other good stuff in there, other deep and meaningful information about yourself that you will find.

As you know, one of my patterns was becoming involved with unavailable men. A quick side-note on availability. My girlfriends and I talk about this all the time; there appears to be some general confusion about how to tell whether or not a person is available. Here are three sure-fire ways to tell that a person is not available.

First, if he doesn't live in the same city as you do, he's not available. I was notorious for "dating" guys long distance from the jump. The internet makes is super easy to do this, but I've got a newsflash for you, if he doesn't live in the same general geographic location as you do, he's not available. People don't begin their relationships long-distance. Mind blown, right? Usually, couples that have been together for more than a hot minute, make the decision to endure a long-distance separation because of some external pressure (a job, or a sick family member, etc.). Starting something out long distance really exacerbates the fantasy aspect of a relationship and in turn; its unsustainability. Flying in and out of town for a weekend, rendezvousing once a month, staying up late chatting or texting on the phone, really *feeling* the "distance makes the heart grow fonder thing," all of this is fun.

But, if your flirtation consists of only this, then it is not grounded in the day to day reality required for building deep and meaningful intimacy with a partner. What do I mean by this? All relationships have that pink-cloud, honeymoon, new love moment stuff. I call this phase cupcaking. Cupcaking is fun, it's important, and it can lead to deep intimacy. But cupcaking alone won't get you there. Intimacy gets built when we share the scary stuff. You know, the stuff that's like "EEEK I don't like that I feel this way, but I do, and I need to let you know about it." Do not skip this uncomfortable stuff. It is truly the only way to bear your soul to another human. Metaphorically, dating long-distance and expecting a deep and intimate relationship is kind of like eating only whipped cream and Snickers bars and expecting a bodybuilder physique.

Second, if he is currently involved with another woman, is separated (not even divorced yet), or is recently divorced (under a year), he's not available. This is a hard and fast rule for me. Listen, I've been divorced, maybe you've been divorced. If you have, then you know, nobody who gets divorced had a super-awesome marriage, because super-awesome marriages don't end in divorce. So. Divorce comes with baggage, and I'm here to tell you, you are not somebody else's baggage claim. A divorced man needs to claim his own damn baggage and work through whatever got his ass divorced before he can be a fully available partner to you. The only thing that mitigates the unavailability of a recent divorce/breakup for me, is if he has been doing growth work (like therapy) around it. But still, proceed with caution. Especially, if dating unavailable men is your thing. It was totally mine.

> Dating long-distance and expecting a deep and intimate relationship is kind of like eating only whipped cream and Snickers bars and expecting a bodybuilder physique.

Third, he's emotionally unavailable. This one can be tricky. To this day, I am better at identifying when he's emotionally unavailable than when he is fully available. For example, if he's 40 and he's still resentful that his mom remarried a jerk after his dad left, and he is carrying that around with him, and telling you about it on one of your first dates, he's not emotionally available. He's not a grown-ass man and he's got some work to do.

I turned to my close friend The Real Sandy J, for her thoughts on the subject as I was prepping this part of the book. As we discussed it, we determined that emotional availability boils down to this: how appropriately does he deal with the stuff that grown people deal with? More particularly, how does he handle life on life's terms? Can he take responsibility or is it always someone else's fault? If he's always the victim, he's emotionally unavailable. Because here's the thing, he may have been a victim, some gnarly shit might have happened to him in his life. But, if he's a man who wants to be available, if he wants to have intimacy and a sustainable romantic relationship, he will have done some work to move through his trauma. He will have found a way to quit blaming his mom.

Emotional availability is really about sharing our authentic selves with our partners. So, if he is unable to tell you that he likes you, if he can't tell you that he loves you, if you can't tell him that you love him because you are afraid of his response, he is not emotionally available. An available man will be able to say to you, "I'm interested in you and I'd like to get to you know you better" and when the time comes, he will be able to say "I love you and I'm not afraid to be vulnerable with you." Or some variation of this. An emotionally available man will be able to hear your feelings and be curious about them. For me, a woman who has a relationship with a man who is emotionally available, I have found that our relationship is grounded in reality. I am willing to share my feelings with him; he is willing and able to share his feelings with me. And, perhaps most importantly, we are curious about each other's feelings.

A word here about alcoholism and addiction. If you are a person who drinks normally or uses drugs casually and you are dating someone whose behavior with regard to substances concerns you, trust your gut. You're probably right and you don't have to go down with someone else's sinking ship. This person is probably very emotional but is very definitely not emotionally available. Take care of yourself and get out while you can.

Some of us grapple with the rather "charming" character defect of laying eyes on an emotionally wounded person and deciding that we can "fix" them. First of all: this is garbage. We are not powerful enough to "fix" anyone. Second, someone who is not willing to work on themselves, absolutely, positively, does not want to be "fixed" by you. Even if, in the beginning, they feign delight about being "fixed," they will undoubtedly grow to resent the overbearingness that comes along with being "fixed" by you. Third, a deeply wounded person, while worthy of love and self-love, is absolutely not available to be in a sustainable relationship with deep and meaningful intimacy.

> **Some of us grapple with the rather "charming" character defect of laying eyes on an emotionally wounded person and deciding that we can "fix" them. First of all. This is garbage.**

You might choose to ignore this entire discussion about availability and decide that you want to become involved with a person who is emotionally unavailable. If you do, I hope you move forward with eyes wide open. An emotionally unavailable person cannot provide the reciprocal love and deep intimacy that a fully available person can. I inevitably found that when I chose to get involved with unavailable men, it was painful. And it hurt more and more each time I did it.

You've made your list, you've identified your patterns, you've looked at how those patterns affect you and what your parts are in them (like maybe you keep selecting unavailable partners).

What's next?

7

THE SPIRITUAL GANGSTER

I was not born a little baby buddha, a spiritual gangster, or a seeker of truth. But today, if someone were asking "Who wants to investigate some spiritual shit?" I'd shoot my hand up in the air and say, "Yep, let's do this!" I am as open minded as I have ever been to teachers, seekers, and concepts. I'm willing to try daily meditation, sleeping meditation, yoga, daily prayer, any number of 12-step guides, crystals, oils, self-help, you name it. I'll try any suggestion that comes from someone *who looks like they have what I want:* long-term relationships, intimacy, emotional stability, and serenity.

I want to challenge you to remain open-minded and to stick with this chapter, even if, *especially if,* all this talk of spirituality, seeking, energy, and truth is making your skin crawl. I found that in order to truly tap into this resource and this journey, I had to set aside my old ideas of God, Spirit, and the Universe.

Prior to hitting an alcoholic bottom and then, in sobriety, hitting a bottom with men and relationships, it never even occurred to me that I might need some help outside of what I could do for myself. I had

> I'll try any suggestion that comes from someone who looks like they have what I want - long-term relationships, intimacy, emotional stability, and serenity.

always been quite capable. Self-help (plus some therapy here or there) had always been enough for me. In all the jams that I had gotten myself in (and believe me there were more than those outlined here), it never occurred to me that I could, or even should, turn my attention to tapping into a universal energy that was conspiring to help me. And it certainly didn't dawn on me that this help could be in whatever form I desired; I was not required to turn to some old white dude in the sky.

The Spirit or God of my youth was that old white dude. I grew up with organized religion. Our family regularly attended a Presbyterian Church. It did always seem a little bit like church-lite, though. Like everyone paid lip service to worship, but we all knew people were really there to just have a good time. All to say, I don't recall a lot of fire and brimstone. Members hosted pool parties every weekend in the summer, we lined the boulevard to cheer on runners during The Bix 7 , there was always food and tailgating for Iowa football games, there were tons of kids to bop around with, and there was a full-size basketball court in the basement of the church.

The incredibly talented Mr. Music was the Minister of Music. Mr. Music was everything. He was tall and slim. He had with blonde hair that never wavered from its style, even when he zipped around in his red Mazda Miata. He was like a magical unicorn in the landscape of my teenage life. He had a charge card with Von Maur (the fanciest department store in the Quad Cities), he only wore Tommy Hilfiger, and he never wore the same outfit twice. There was even a rumor that he had a conveyor belt in his closet, that his outfits could be ordered up on demand like at the dry-cleaner or like Cher's closet in the movie Clueless.

> Mr. Music was everything. He was tall and slim. He had with blonde hair that never wavered from its style, even when he zipped around in his red Mazda Miata.

Mr. Music demanded excellence from his musicians, but I was delighted by this because I loved to sing and I felt like when I was in his choir, I was singing with the best. This was, of course, confirmed when our Junior Choir was selected to sing back up for Barry Manilow when he came to town.[14]   Under Mr. Music's guidance, our little church choir staged performances of *Les Miserables, Fiddler on the Roof, Godspell, Into the Woods, The Music Man* and many others.

There was community and there was music. What more could I ask for? If it meant I had to endure a little Sunday School here and there, an occasional bible story, yeah, I could swing that. This place was my island, a little oasis in the chaos of my life. I loved it. Whereas I felt alienated as school, I felt at home in this spot. When the kids at school thought I was weird, I felt valued by these people. When I second guessed myself relentlessly at school. I felt confident with this community. I felt safe.

My parents were active members of this congregation, they were choir members, they had been cast in these musicals, they were regulars at the tailgates and parties. And then one day, it all changed. My mother and I had attended Good Friday services, we both sang in the choir that evening. As I ran down the church steps, my mother came up them. I told her I was off to go see a movie with some friends (Spiceworld). She said she was headed out with hers. I got home later that evening and my dad mentioned that my mom wasn't home yet, but he wanted my friends and I out of the house. I wanted to keep flirting with a boy that had caught my attention, so we went and hung out at some park. My mom arrived back home before I did, so when I came home, I went to bed.

The next morning, I woke up late for work. "Shit!" I scrambled down the stairs. My dad was at the kitchen table, my mom was on the couch. Unusual. "Mom, are you Ok?" Slowly, she replied, "No, honey, I'm not." "Make sure you talk to dad about it, I'm late for work." I was out the door, into my little black Pontiac, off to my hostessing job at Cheddars. My dad called me an hour later. They were in the ER. My mom had come home the night before and taken every pill she could find. She had tried to kill herself. This wasn't the turning point for me with God, it was what came next.

---

[14] I wanted to include the picture that I have of this little choir posing with Mr. Manilow, but it required a LOT of signed releases. So, if you want to see it, email me. I got you, boo. Needless to say, Mr. Manilow wore a teal jacket, and sported, what at the time seemed like, a particularly aggressive spray tan. And I am front and center. Just how I like it.

My mother had taken an overdose and she spent the weekend in ICU. It was Easter weekend. I felt untethered, like I was walking around outside of my body. I didn't know what to do with myself. So, on Sunday, I went to church. I sat in the congregation, in a spot near the front. And I was alone. I went to the service alone, I sat alone, and after it was done, I was still alone. All the choir members knew what had happened, long-time family friends were aware. And yet. Only one woman, a woman who I didn't know very well at all, approached me and asked if I was Ok. This community, these people, had abandoned me. It was more than I could bear. Within days, it seemed, my mother had abandoned me, my community had abandoned me, my Spirit, my Universal Power, my God had left me high and dry. I was devastated. It was years before I could set foot in church without crying.

I can acknowledge that I wish this had gone differently.

I wish I had been embraced.

I wish I had felt comforted.

I wish I had felt carried.

Ultimately, I felt disappointed by the humanness of these people. Disappointed, hurt, and wounded. And I used their humanness to discount religion, and I used religion to discount spirituality. What I have discovered in the aftermath is this: humans are just that, human. Putting anyone on a pedestal will leave me disappointed. A Universal Spirit didn't let me down that day, humans did. And, eventually, I found some compassion for them. How strange it must have been, the sight of me, alone, that morning? Maybe people were confused, maybe they didn't know what to say, maybe they felt guilty or overwhelmed. But I had a part in my own experience too, I expected that they would read my mind and I didn't know how to ask for what I needed.

Eventually, my mom was cleared out of ICU and she entered a 28-day treatment program. She got sober and stayed sober and today she has over 21 years of continuous sobriety. And when I needed to get sober, I knew what to do because of the example that she set for me. And what a blessing that was. Only something as powerful as the universe could have orchestrated such an experience.

This experience, where I became so disappointed in my faith, happened when I was 17. I didn't return to relying on Spirit, or the Universe, or God until I was 31. So, there were 14 intervening years where I really got used to being completely and totally self-reliant. I was just charging right through my life, reins in hand, high-stepping all over the landscape. I've always been incredibly driven, I fancied myself as self-sufficient (and, to some extent, I was, although I did have the privilege of parents who were able to help me out when I was in a jam), I was organized and stubborn and generally able to power through a lot of stuff. I felt like, "Yeah, I have my shit on lock." But, as far as my relationships were concerned, the old patterns and old behaviors (that I had identified in the list) were running the show. I needed to try something different. I needed to find some humility to accept that the Universe might have a different plan for me. I started to ask for help and I'm going to ask you to do that too.

I can acknowledge that I wish this had gone differently.

I wish I had been embraced.

I wish I had felt comforted.

I wish I had felt carried.

How did I reconnect with the Spirit of the Universe, when I felt so jilted? Well, my relationship with the Universe has evolved over time. First, I just accepted and acknowledged that there were powers out there that were (1) not me and (2) bigger than me. So, I was like, "You know, nature is pretty powerful and pretty big. If a helicopter flew me out over an ocean and the co-pilot opened the little sliding door and kicked me out of the back, I would be totally fucked. I guess, eventually, I would either drown or a shark would come eat me. So, in a very real sense, either the Ocean or a Shark are both more powerful than me." This was an admittedly dark perspective.

But it worked. It gave me some open-mindedness, and eventually, my perspective about powers greater than myself shifted.

The ocean and sharks were two things that I considered more powerful than myself. And I rolled with that when I attended my girlfriend Amme's wedding. Amme married her sweetheart, Mike, on the Oregon coast. Amme and Mike were both scooter enthusiasts. Most of the people in attendance were part of this scooter-crew and they partied hard. I was sober, but I remember watching several bottles of fireball make their way through the crowd as they said their "I do's." With everyone lit before the end of the ceremony, things really kicked into high gear when Amme's father introduced some kind of Greek liquor (maybe moonshine Sambuca?) to the guests at the reception. It was loud, it was jubilant, it was chaos.

Amid all that chaos, I stood back and looked around, honestly, I was thinking, "FML, how am I gonna stay here another minute and not drink?" And there, in the corner of the reception hall, my gaze fell on a set of new parents just completely enthralled with their tiny baby. They were both holding her, and they were looking down on her little face. They were immune from the noise and the chaos; it was as if the three of them were in their own little world. And suddenly, I got it. I understood the concept of a power greater than myself. I was struck by the power of love.

You know, nature is pretty powerful and pretty big. If a helicopter flew me out over an ocean and the co-pilot opened the little sliding door and kicked me out of the back, I would be totally fucked. I guess, eventually, I would either drown or a shark would come eat me. So, in a very real sense, either the Ocean or a Shark are both more powerful than me.

As I watched those two watching their baby. My thoughts turned to my own parents. And I realized that it didn't matter what kind of shitty shit I had done. And it didn't matter what kind of shitty shit they had done. I was sure that they had looked at me in this way. I knew, deeply, that the power of love was unlimited and unconditional. I became acutely aware of my belief in the power of love. This was such a powerful experience for me. And that's just it, it's mine. The point isn't that you'll have the same experience - your parents might have done some unforgivable shitty shit, or they might not have done any shitty shit, whatever - the point is that you'll have an experience that changes your perspective on Universal Energy, God, or Spirit.

When I finally bottomed out with men and relationships, I had to ask myself some tough questions. How could I believe in the pervasiveness of the power of love, and yet, exclude it from my own love life? How could I trust and really accept the power of love as an unlimited source of energy conspiring for great things and yet push it away when it came to romantic love for me? Keeping it at arm's length with a very polite, "Nothing to see here, I've got this, thankyouverymuch." I found that I had to start turning to this power, in order to receive guidance and direction, in the form of intuitive thought and awareness, in my experiences with men and relationships. And honestly, it felt gangster. When I turn to the Universe and ask it for help, I can let go of a lot of the micromanaging of my life. When I'm inviting this power in, I know that it's got my back. So, my job is to just show up in my life as a human and to honor my Truth the best that I can. Then the Universe takes care of the rest. I put in the hustle, and the Universe takes care of the outcome. And when I'm in this flow, I feel free.

The next bit is a daily practice. Turn to whatever you are willing to believe in (love, God, a higher power, the universe, big mama, nature, sharks, the ocean, the forest, an ancestor) and begin to ask for some help. Ask even if you haven't had a connection with this power in a while. Ask even if you've never asked it for anything before. Ask even if you haven't asked it for anything since you begged for Doc Martens when you were 13 but didn't get them and so you stopped asking. Ask it even if you have felt disappointed by it before. Begin now to turn to it and simply thank it for the newfound awareness you have of these patterns and ask for the willingness to behave differently. Try it out for two weeks, just see how it feels. If it feels good, keep doing it beyond the two weeks, if it doesn't, then don't.

You can also enlist your friends in this endeavor. In order to get through this, I had to talk about it with my friends a lot. And think about it, your friends just want the opportunity to get to know you better and they want you to be happy. So, share what you can with your friends. When you've identified some patterns that you don't want to engage in, tell your friends about them. Ask them if they will be willing to call you out when they see

> When I finally bottomed out with men and relationships, I had to ask myself some tough questions. How could I believe in the pervasiveness of the power of love and, yet, exclude it from my own love life?

you engaging in these old behaviors. I bet they will. Keep in mind, that you've asked them to do this; so, don't be mad at them (for too long) when they call you out on your bullshit.

8

STEP INTO YOUR POWER

Many of the patterns that I identified with "The List" were patterns of behavior that were driven by fear. So, it's really important to acknowledge what those fears are. Now, I'm going to ask you to make a list of all your fears as they relate to personal relationships. These fears can be deep or superficial, silly or serious, as long as they are really yours. For example, one of my fears was that I was afraid that while I was doing this work, I would get fat, and no one would find me attractive. I mean, seriously, how basic? But that was a fear that was eating my lunch.

I had been overweight as a kid and I hadn't done much dating or been on the receiving end of much attention. Then, suddenly, in my early thirties, I had become confident and quite active and I received a ton of attention from men. And it felt good, like really fucking good. But this old fear cut deep. What if I stopped running 40 miles a week because I wasn't training for a marathon anymore? What would happen to my body? And weren't my legs my money makers? What would happen if my muffin top came back? I spent a lot of time in the body-image rabbit hole. This obsession (and that is absolutely what it was) with self-worth determined by male attention and body image had to go; it was painful and unsustainable. But I didn't know how to get rid of it.

When I did all the exercises that I've outlined here, I started to accept and love me. I started to realize that I am Ok, whether I have admirers or not. That I am more than relationships and attention from men. That I am a fucking woman and I am not defined by any of this shit. And then I stepped into my power. Annnnnnnd then I gave it up again. So much of my journey—in life, in sobriety, in relationships—has been about discovering my truth and stepping into my power. Then getting scared and giving it back up to play small. Then becoming aware of what I have done, getting honest with myself and another human being and, stepping back in to my power. The exciting thing about this tug-of-war, is that every time I chose to step back into it, every time I chose to honor my capital-T TRUTH and accept who I am, my power gets bigger. I get

These fears can be deep or superficial, silly or serious, as long as they are really yours.

more authentic, I get more powerful and that, *that*, is extraordinary.

Another fear that I wrote down was this; I was afraid that if I was honest with my partner about my feelings, that realness would be overwhelming to someone else. I was always afraid that if I had any feelings at all and *dared* to express them, that I would be considered drama. So, for years I pushed my feelings down and pretended to be the "cool girl" where nothing mattered, nothing was triggering, and nothing got under my skin. But do you know what did happen? I lost myself and I was miserable. And when I was being the "cool girl" I wasn't able to make authentic or intimate connections with the people around me. When I finished this work, I was literally begging the universe to help me to not pretend to be the cool girl anymore.

In an effort to avoid being "drama," I began to accept all kinds of unacceptable behavior from men. If we had plans, but I didn't hear from him about any specifics until 8:30 p.m. that day, I would respond with, "oh yeah, cool, yeah no worries, sure let's meet up at 10 p.m., whatever's clever." Today, I would find something like this situation unacceptable, but both he and I have a part to own for the outcome. First let's start with me. My unacceptable behavior in this situation was not honoring my truth.

More often than not, I would have been waiting around to hear from this guy. You know, arranging my schedule around these mystery plans, getting anxious about not hearing from him and having feelings about it. But, because I was afraid of being drama or afraid that this guy would consider me a bitch, I would just say "whatever." When my heart was asking me to say, "I think it's rude that I didn't hear from you, so I'm not interested in going out with you tonight" instead. An even simpler form of this is; "That hurt my feelings, and this doesn't meet my needs, so I think we're done here."

As for his part, dudes, this is rude and unacceptable behavior. If you want to go out with someone, commit and make plans when you make the date. When you refuse or are unwilling to actually nail down a date, time, and place for a commitment ahead of time, the implication is that you do not value the other person's time or schedule. This is actually a really important reminder for all of us. Being respectful of one another is critical to demonstrating our value to each other.

> In an effort to avoid being "drama," I began to accept all kinds of unacceptable behavior from men.

Another manifestation of the "cool girl" syndrome (for me) was being willing to settle as someone's side piece. I found myself in any number of personnel configurations whereby I was the other woman. I discussed this at length earlier—as it pertained to unavailability—but I'd like to revisit it here. I regularly lied to myself about how it felt to be in this role. When I break stuff down like this, I like to think of myself as a pie chart. When I found myself in relationships with men who were in relationships with other women, I know that a large slice of me felt comfortable with this because I was protected by their unavailability. I did not have to be truly vulnerable with them because they were unavailable to me. But another slice of me felt like being in relationships with men who were in relationships with other women facilitated my sexual empowerment. And so, I took on a role of, *I do what I want, I fuck who I want, and I don't care what anyone has to say about it.* If this had really been my capital-T TRUTH, then that would have been fine. But this was not my capital-T TRUTH, it was a lie that I was telling myself in order to justify sleeping with men who were in relationships with other women. But you know, I didn't know it was a lie, until I did, and then I had to start do something different.

Letting this "cool girl" persona thing go sounds like Growing Up 101, but it took me forever to learn. It is one of the things that I still struggle with today. Learning to identify feelings and the needs that go along with them is a grown-ass woman thing to do. For me, communicating these feelings required an entire paradigm shift in my thinking. I had to learn that communicating my real feelings (and their attendant needs) to my partner was a requirement

> I took on a role of, like, I do what I want, I fuck who I want, and I don't care what anyone has to say about it.

of building deep and meaningful intimacy. In fact, deep intimacy can't be built on the denial of feelings or the unwillingness to be fully honest about our Capital-T Truths. I had to become willing trust that my relationships were resilient and that they could withstand the expression of my actual feelings. In fact, intimacy demands this. I began to accept that relationships that disintegrated when I expressed my feelings were not healthy or intimate relationships in the first place. I adopted the mantra, *if you can't handle my feelings*, you can't roll with me. And I started to live it.

Another big fear on my list: I was afraid that if I wasn't always the center of attention that people would forget about me. This was about my self-worth being defined by attention from men, and largely about my sense of self being validated by the attention of others. This fear of turning into wallpaper (which as you recall, used to be a goal of mine) is completely egocentric. I had always known, logically, that I am not what others think of me, but I had never deeply accepted that, because attention felt so good!

Male attention, in particular, was so valuable to me. I had never taken a legit break from dating (like I did for the eleven months that it took me to do this work), so I had never taken the opportunity to evaluate the real effect of my desire for male attention on my soul or on my behaviors. When I decided to step off the dating merry-go-round for nearly a year, I was able to finally see just how my compulsion around male attention was affecting me. And how, you might ask, was that? Well, my constant desire for attention made all of my relationships unsustainable. For two reasons; (1) no man could provide me the sustained level of attention that I required, and (2) the grass was always greener. The desire for attention from new players in the game always trumped the attention from someone I was already seeing. I was easily distracted by bright, shiny, objects. Attention was like a drug and I was a junkie, sacrificing my values, treating people like playthings, and constantly chasing that high.

When I did this work, I discovered that none of that attention had ever provided me with anything fulfilling in my life. It didn't serve me. It wasn't generous, or loving, or kind. It was not abundant or fruitful. It was hollow and empty. I had to set attention and attention-seeking down. These tools lost their spots in the toolkit. When I accepted that I could step away from the attention drug, my relationships almost immediately improved. I wasn't so quick to fall victim to the "grass is always greener" narrative that had run on loop in my brain. I learned to take the time to go out on a date with someone, to get some information about them and to make a decision about whether or not I wanted to learn more about them. Then I got to go out on another date with them and I got to get more information and I got to re-evaluate and decide again, whether or not I wanted to see them again and get more information. This process of information gathering, evaluation, re-evaluation, and decision making was so much more measured and sustainable than the constant attention-seeking that had dominated my life.

My fears don't have to be your fears. You might identify with them, you might be intrigued by them, you might even be repulsed by them. But I'm sharing them with you to demonstrate what it's like to get honest about our fears. To show you what this work helped me grow through and to inspire you to get honest with yourself about the deep-rooted fears you have about men, relationships, and yourself.

My constant desire for attention made all of my relationships unsustainable.

Once you've got all of your fears written down, ask yourself, how effective has your approach to alleviating these fears been? Even with therapy, I hadn't made much headway on mine all by myself. When I really stopped to look at this list of fears, I realized I'd been carrying some for them around for decades. In the last chapter I asked you to consider a power greater than yourself. I asked you to find some willingness to begin communicating with the Universal Energy around you, to begin to find some open-mindedness around the accessibility of Great Spirit. Now, I'm going to ask you to consider giving these fears to that power. But what would that look like? Well, I'm glad you asked.

There are a couple of concrete things you can do to turn these fears over. First, if you're into ritual, you can easily develop a ritual for this. For example, I know a woman who wrote each of her fears on rocks and then ceremoniously threw each rock in a fast-moving river. You could also burn your fears list. You can create a little box or container to hold your fears and you can put them all in there. You can burn some sage; you can light some incense. You get the idea. When you develop a ritual, you get the experience of physically and symbolically washing your hands of these fears.

Some spiritual paths refer to these as character defects, I sometimes think of them as character defenses. For a long time, these tools helped me navigate a world that was challenging for me to understand. And before they started to hurt me, they had helped me.

Also, if you're vibing on talking to this new power you're working with, you can try to integrate turning these fears over into your prayer work. Don't overthink this. Prayer work is just the conversation that you're having with The Universe, Spirit, God, Nature, Love or whatever. Personally, I use this prayer all the time and it helps me to remember that I'm Ok, no matter what fears I'm having.[15] So, I will say, "Take me to a place where my

---

[15] I cannot take credit for this prayer. It is a tool that I gleaned from recovery and although, to my knowledge it was never published, my first exposure to it was in

relationship with _____ is less important than my relationship with you." I fill in the blank with whatever fear I'm having. For example, "Take me to a place where my relationship with Mr. Husband is less important than my relationship with you," or "Take me to a place where my relationship with my body is less important than my relationship with you." When I am done with this (it is scary to do at first), I have turned my fears over in a very meaningful way.

After you've got this list of fears (but before you burn them in ritual!), see if you can dig a little deeper. See if you are willing to also list what part of your character they are related to. So for me, my fear of getting fat was related to how I see myself (my ego), how I want others to see me (my sense of pride), and self-centeredness (obsessing about how other people might see me, think of me, or remember me). My fear around my authentic self as too overwhelming for someone else was also related to my ego and pride. And, behavior -wise, it manifested in my life as dishonesty in my relationships.

These underlying aspects of character (pride, self-centeredness, ego,) can all be removed or diminished when we stop practicing them regularly in our relationships. I found that as I stopped being dishonest, honesty began to come more naturally. As I stopped caring what others thought about me—I did this at first by just pretending that I had a set of horse blinders on—pride mattered less.

My job was to stop practicing these things that caused me pain, and eventually, the universe took them out of my arsenal as my first-strike tools. So basically, I stopped engaging in my go-to behaviors. I paused before I was dishonest about my feelings and found some willingness to be honest instead. At this stage, dishonesty was still my number one go-to, but the universe provided me enough grace to (1) feel the dishonesty coming, (2) pause before I opened my mouth, and (3) say something honest instead. After practicing this type of contrary action for a while (a long time, probably at least a year or so), Great Spirit eventually shifted my thinking so that my first thought was honesty about my feelings instead of dishonesty.

the Judge John workbook study of the Big Book of Alcoholics Anonymous.

Some spiritual paths refer to these as character defects; but I've also heard them called character defenses, which I like. For a long time, these tools helped me navigate a world that was challenging for me to understand. And before they started to hurt me, they had helped me. But, by the time I was willing to set them down, they weren't helping me anymore. It was time to expand on the tools that I had and to pick up some new tools along the way: integrity, honesty, tolerance, love, and service.

9

FIND YOU, FIND YOUR CREW

By this stage, you've taken a good, hard look at yourself. You've identified some patterns in your relationships and, more importantly, you've identified your part in those patterns. You've started working on developing a relationship with some kind of power to help you with this that includes enlisting some friends to hold you accountable.

In the last chapter, I asked you to start turning to either this power (Higher Power, God, Spirit, Big Mama, your friends) to change your behavior. I asked you to do this because, in order to change my relationship patterns, I had to stop engaging in that old, defense-mechanism behavior (i.e. being the "cool girl," being manipulative, selecting unavailable partners, etc.). The good news is, once I developed the habit of behaving in a new way, my thoughts eventually followed. What I mean is that; when I started showing up to my relationships in an authentic way, my brain/thoughts were screaming at me, "This is scary!! What are you doing!! Don't do this!!" But I ignored my brain and was authentic anyway. Eventually, my brain and thoughts got used to the idea of authenticity and they didn't throw a temper tantrum every single time I was authentic and vulnerable.[16]

---

[16] Although I will admit, they are having a field day with this project.

I truly believe that the best way to find a new way of thinking is to act your way into it. In other words, I have never been capable of thinking myself into a new way of acting. The more I think about something, the more I double-down. I recommit to the behavior that I've always done and that I'm so sure about. And the results inevitably leave me disappointed. So, let's flip this on its head. Let's act our way into a new way of thinking with regard to these relationship patterns and old defense-mechanism behaviors.

> Eventually, my brain and thoughts got used to the idea of authenticity and they didn't throw a temper tantrum every single time I was authentic and vulnerable.

The next exercise is called "I Am/ I Desire." I've provided pages at the end of this book for this exercise. Make two columns:

1. I am confident in
2. I desire confidence in

Fill in your columns. Be honest, what are you supremely confident in. In what areas are you the baddest bitch you know? Write those down, lean into them, own them. They are yours, you have earned them, you have decided them, nothing can change them. As far as the "I desire" column, give it some real thought. What do you desire confidence in? If you wanted something different for your life, what would you need to achieve that?

This exercise is about stepping into your power and womanhood. What kind of woman do you want to be? I'll tell you about the kind of woman I thought I was and the kind I thought I wanted to be. I didn't have much listed in the "I am confident in" column. I listed the following: (1) I am confident in my "look good," (2) I am confident in my sense of humor, (3) I am confident in my ability to make other people feel good, (4) I am confident in my ability to speak to a room.

I want to acknowledge that when I did this exercise, I only found four things that I was confident in. I am telling you, I wracked my brain, I thought and thought about this and I could only muster these four things. And two of the four (half!) are related to external motivators, with one related to how well I hid my authentic self (look good) and the other to how well I supported and took care of others.

My "look good" was the way that I showed up in the world. And when my "look good" is reflective of who I am, it's just me being authentic. But when my "look good" doesn't match who I am, it's dangerous, it's inauthentic and it's exhausting. Because "look good" that isn't aligned with who I am is just another form of dishonesty. Social media is a great mirror for "look good." Some of us do a great job of maintaining consistency between social media and real life. Some of us, not so much. My job today is to be authentic as I can be, to show up as myself in all areas of my life, including social media. When I finished all this work, I realized that my "look good" was harming me because it was inauthentic and inconsistent with who I really was. It was going to be necessary for me to show up to my life in a more authentic and vulnerable way. To let go of the "look good," the smiles for everyone, the obsession over every hair and eyelash, and to embrace the good enough.

While these character traits (good sense of humor, care-taking, great public speaking skills) are awesome, I wasn't sure that they were the bedrock on which a sustainable relationship could be built. As I stared down that "I Am Confident In" list, it didn't look pretty. How in the world, was I going to become a woman who was capable of sustainable, romantic, love?! That is what the "I Desire" side of the exercise was for.

Tackling the "I Desire" side of this list is an exercise in no-limit thinking. Don't limit yourself to things you think are reasonable or things that you think others would expect of you. Consider your list of fears, consider the patterns you've identified, consider the woman that you want to become and consider what that would really take. Then fill in the "I Desire" side.

The first thing on my "I Desire" list was the ability to be honest about my feelings. I had spent my entire life managing the way I expressed my feelings in order to manipulate your response to them. It meant that I was constantly walking on eggshells, rarely able to express what was in my heart.

I just knew that if I did, you would react to me in a way that would make me uncomfortable. So, you see, I was always managing your reaction to me instead of surfacing toward you with my authentic self. Learning to be honest about my feelings has taken a long time. I practiced this behavior with women who were my friends long before I was able to practice it in my relationships with men. I learned that in order for me to feel comfortable being honest about my feelings, I had to first trust that I was in a resilient relationship. I had to trust that my relationships (platonic or romantic) could withstand my honesty. I had to admit that I just wasn't management material, and then I had to quit managing my feelings and just show up with them.

I also listed that I desired a quiet confidence. I was ready to build a sense of self that was not dependent on being the center of attention. I was ready to believe that I would continue to exist, even if I wasn't the center of attention. The willingness to develop this quiet confidence really emerged when I bottomed out with my attention seeking behavior. As I did The List work, and I found myself writing the phrase "attention-seeking" over and over again, I was able to acknowledge the pain that this "grass is always greener" approach had truly caused me. I found I had to change this attention-seeking, self-centered behavior.

Tackling the "I Desire" side of this list is an exercise in no-limit thinking.

I did a couple of things. I began to ask the universe to make me of maximum service to the people around me. Then, I started practicing this with my girlfriends, and I became curious. When I showed up to hang out with them, I started by asking them about their lives, instead of launching into my own. When I met new people, I asked questions. Did they live in the area? How long had they lived here? How did they know the host? How did they find out about the event? What kind of projects were they working on? Did they know how to knit? Without feeling comfortable doing it at all, I found some willingness to shift my behavior from self-centered attention whore to curious and inquisitive party guest. Eventually, the universe shifted my perspective and this behavior became second nature to me.

I've been talking about willingness a lot. I want you to understand that willingness is not the same thing as wanting-ness. It's easy to be willing to do something when I want to do it. When somebody asks me to do something that I am pretty stoked to do in the first place, I consider that wanting-ness. But, when someone suggests I do something that I do not want to do and I find the wherewithal to do it anyway, that is willingness. I have really only experienced true willingness three times in my life: when I got sober, when I did this work around men and relationships, and when I shifted my behavior from self-centered to other-centered.

The next thing on my "I Desire" list was the ability to self-soothe. I found that I was really good at taking care of other people, but that I was not great at taking care of myself. As I tried to navigate the best way to do self-care, I discovered that I didn't know myself very well. Kind of like Julia Roberts in the movie Runaway Bride, remember that one? In the movie, Julia Roberts plays a woman named Maggie who has been engaged like a zillion times, but she just can't ever make it down the aisle on her big day. Part of the plot line is that Maggie adjusts her interests to be consistent with those of her fiancé, this is most notably reflected in the way she eats her eggs. Always in the same way that her fiancé eats them. Richard Gere's character[17]—Ike, brings this to her attention and challenges her about how she really likes her eggs. It's cliché, it's cheesy, it's embarrassing, but for me it was true. I didn't know how I liked my (metaphorical) eggs.

> I want you to understand that willingness is not the same thing as wanting-ness. It's easy to be willing to do something when I want to do it.

So, for me, self-care started with asking myself, "What do I even like?" Did I like hiking? No. Did I like camping? Hell no. As a long-time resident of the Pacific Northwest, it came as quite a shock to me (and to a lot of people

---

[17] Sidebar, I mean—God is there, like, a more loveable duo than Richard Gere and Julia Roberts? Why can't they just be married in real life?

around me) to discover that I prefer a shopping mall and an ice-cold Diet Coke to roughing it out in the woods. I am a child of the 90s. I will not apologize for my love of the American shopping mall. I just won't. I like having my nails done. I love being in the city. I'd rather get audited by the IRS than spend the weekend in the wilderness.

Once I got comfortable with finding out the things I liked and didn't like, it became easier to exercise self-care and self-soothing when I needed it. Subsequently, I was able to focus internally when I didn't feel well, rather than focus externally in order to manage someone else. This was one that I really had to practice with a romantic partner, and I probably practiced it the most with Mr. Husband. Mr. Husband has a great sense of boundaries and he did a great job of helping me to notice when I was feeling agitated and started trying to manage him. He would delicately, like, Keanu-Reeves-attempting-to-defuse-the-bomb-under-the-bus-in-the-movie-Speed-level-delicately, point it out to me and eventually, I learned how to spot it for myself. It's my job to soothe myself, not to soothe anybody else.

> I am a child of the 90s, I will not apologize for my love of the American shopping mall. I just won't. I like having my nails done, I love being in the city. I'd rather get audited by the IRS than spend the weekend in the wilderness.

The point of this "I Am/ I Desire" exercise (although I'm not sure it's necessary to *understand* why you're doing it; just *do it*), is to acknowledge how amazing and confident you already are and to outline a set of ideals to help you move closer toward the woman you want to become. At this stage, Ms. Warrior Spirit told me to start collecting women who had the confidence in the things to which I aspired. No, she was not referring to collecting women in like a "put the lotion in the basket" kind of way (Silence of the Lambs, anyone?). She was referring to the power of the people that we choose to surround ourselves with. If I wanted to be a woman who ran my own company, I needed to put a few of those in my network. If I wanted to be a woman who valued fitness, I needed to make friends with some women who also valued fitness.

This was a big ask. Huge. Almost as big as asking me to refrain from one on one contact with men. I thought, damn, haven't I already done enough? I told her, "But, I'm a guy's girl, I'm not friends with women."

Let's take a minute - a quick digression if you will - to discuss this phenomenon, The Guy's Girl. You've probably met this woman and actually, if you're doing this work, it's highly probable that you are this woman. This is the woman that says "Omg, girls are so petty and such drama. All my best friends are guys, they are just so much more laid back." I can be snarky about this because I absolutely was this girl. And do you know why I liked attention from guys? And being friends with guys? It was most certainly not because they weren't drama. It was because they had dicks. And I liked attention from those with dicks. Being a guy's girl was a convenient and socially acceptable way for me to surround myself with men and to bask in their attention.

Back to what happened to me when I finally yielded to this completely outrageous request. Spoiler: everything turned out fine *because I was still not talking to men*. So, even though women had never been my first choice, I had no other people in my life to chat with and, miraculously, I became friends with some women. Some real ride-or-die chicks. Women who walk through the shit with me every damn day. Women who I can call when my ass is falling off. Women who have helped me navigate the death of friends and family. Women who kept me grounded as I struggled to navigate the complexity of a blended family. Women who put their hands on my back and said, "Girl, we've got you."

"Omg, girls are so petty and such drama. All my best friends are guys, they are just so much more laid back." Ok, so I can be snarky about this because I absolutely was this girl. And do you know why I liked attention from guys? And being friends with guys? It was most certainly not because they weren't drama, it was because they had dicks.

So, now is the time to start collecting some women. How, exactly, did I do this? Anytime I ran into someone that I knew I wanted to hang with, I said, "You know what? We should get coffee!" and then she would say something like, "Oh yeah, totally!" and then I would go ahead and pull my phone out and say "Great, let's put something on the calendar right now." This is an assertive strategy and, honestly, it's the simplest form of the truth for me. Whatever you do, make sure you do everything you can to avoid the "we should get together someday" trap. Because the point is not to just talk about doing it someday, but to put some energy into these relationships today.

10

YOU GOTTA FORGIVE YOURSELF

One thing about old patterns - they're not old behaviors if you're still doing them. This is, of course, both accurate and infuriating. Sometimes this trite little saying is useful to me, it reminds me about the progress I'm making. Sometimes, I find it so annoying that I want to wail on a mattress with an old tennis racket. I want you to take a look back at your big list, "The List." Pull out all the major patterns, consolidate them, and keep them on your radar.

I'm going to ask you to use what you've learned about your patterns to forgive yourself for the old wreckage, the pain, the sabotage, the harm, the neglect that you've endured. You might be asking yourself, "But how? What does awareness of my patterns have to do with forgiving myself and moving on?" The best way that I know how to move through pain and to heal is to start by stopping the pain. That means I use my awareness of these patterns to avoid engaging in them in the future.

Choosing to behave differently has become one of the most genuine expressions of self-love for me. I will be the first to say that even after doing all this work, I am not always willing to choose differently. But, the majority of the time I do. And even better, when I decide not to choose differently and I do engage in these old behaviors, it doesn't take long for me to see them, to be pained by them, and to initiate a course correction. The reason that I think that this is totally life changing and miraculous, is that prior to completing this work, I wasn't willing to do something different until I was in so much pain that I either wanted to drink or to die. So today, that I only experience a little emotional pain before I'm willing to course correct, is totally a W in my win column.

One thing about old patterns - they're not old behaviors if you're still doing them.

I used the program of work that I've outlined here to forgive myself and to heal by setting aside my old patterns of behavior and by consciously choosing to engage in some new ones. But this is really only half of the equation; these new behaviors were helping to move forward, but I needed a way to forgive myself for the past. What does that mean? I looked at my behavior patterns and I acknowledged that not only had I caused harm to the men with whom I had been involved, but I had also harmed myself.

When I looked at my patterns and relationships and thought about the harm I'd caused, I really only had 2 reactions. For some of those exes, I was chomping at the bit to go hunt him down, to make a coffee date with him in order to "make things right," and, to show him just how well I was doing since we had broken up. For others, I was cowering in a corner trying to make myself invisible because the thought of ever facing him again was too much to bear.

If you're having the second reaction, I have good news for you; you are not to go find every old boyfriend, dredge up each old relationship, and grovel for forgiveness. If you were having the first reaction; sorry (grimace face) but you are not to go find every old boyfriend, dredge up each old relationship and show him how well you're doing without him. While this work did give me some new clarity on these old patterns and relationships, it didn't give me the right to go back and unload all that stuff on to those exes. I didn't get to unburden my own soul and conscious by burdening theirs. In this work, the path to forgiveness and freedom was in the living amend. And I found I had to make a living amend to myself and to these exes.

So, what are living amends? Let's start with differentiating between an amend and an apology. I have come to understand an amend to mean that I have amended my behavior. When I make an apology to someone, I make a verbal acknowledgement of the harm that I caused. But, when I make an amend, I have done an additional level of work, I have practiced doing the opposite of the behavior that caused harm. For example, if my dishonesty caused harm in a relationship, I make an amend by practicing honesty. And I keep practicing honesty until it becomes a consistent behavior, until my dishonest behavior has been amended or transformed to honest behavior. Then if I ever get to a place where I am making a face to face amend to someone, by that stage I will be able to say, "I'm sorry that my dishonesty caused you harm. Today, I practice honesty in my life and I'm not a dishonest person anymore. Thank you for giving me the opportunity to make this right."

> I have good news for you; you are not to go find every old boyfriend, dredge up each old relationship, and grovel for forgiveness.

I was instructed to look at my old behaviors, to examine my part in those relationship patterns and to make a list of things that I didn't want to do in future relationships. I'd be making a living amends to those exes by not treating future relationships in the same way, and I'd be making amends to myself because I would no longer be engaging in that painful, self-harming, self-sabotaging behavior.

My list was simple and looked something like this:

Behaviors to avoid in future relationships

Manipulation and Dishonesty

In my experience, manipulation and dishonesty popped up in my relationships as denial of self; pretending to be something that I wasn't in order to keep someone around. I had to start getting real in my relationships, and I had to start getting comfortable with myself. I did a lot of practice on this one with other women in my life before I was able to practice it in a relationship with a man. But I am so glad that I logged all those moments of honesty because, while it didn't exactly become second nature (it can still be really uncomfortable), it did become my new standard practice. And it means that when shit hits the fan with Mr. Husband today, I have practiced surfacing with my feelings and telling him where I'm at. I want to assure you, there is no perfect way to do this.

If Mr. Husband has had an interaction with (let's be honest) another woman and I feel threatened about it, instead of pretending to be the Cool Girl and acting like nothing matters, I'll usually say "Mr. Husband, I'm really uncomfortable right now and I really wish I didn't feel this way, that's just my truth, it might not be yours, but I am feeling threatened and I need to talk about it with you." I always get embarrassed when I feel threatened or jealous. For me, the most honest way to have a conversation with Mr. Husband about those feelings is to also own how uncomfortable I am about having them; acknowledging that I struggle with accepting that part of my humanity, and that I often wish I didn't feel the way that I do. Communicating this way works really well for me, but it might not for you, so if it doesn't then I would encourage you to take inspiration from the stuff that resonates and to ignore the stuff that doesn't.

I've discovered that showing up authentically to my relationship and communicating with Mr. Husband are the only ways that I can build and nurture deep intimacy in my relationship. It is the scariest shit I have ever done. But every time I do it, each challenging conversation we make it through, reminds me that our relationship is resilient. And that it requires that we both put our full humanity on display: good stuff, weird stuff, neuroses, compulsions, distorted perception, all of it.

Attention-seeking from unavailable men & being the "other woman"

When I started doing all this work, this was by far the most challenging piece of the puzzle. I spent about eleven months doing the writing and exercises that are outlined here and for the entire time I refrained from engaging in one on one contact with men. When I was finished, I started dating. I trusted myself to eliminate suitors that were clearly unavailable, i.e. involved with another woman, lived out of state, or had just gotten out of a LTR. But I was unsure about determining the availability of men who were more in the gray area. So, you know what I did? I started asking my girlfriends for their thoughts on particular men. Because I had been building my crew while I had been on the man-detox program, I had plenty of ladies in my corner who I trusted to weigh in on these dudes.

> I've discovered that showing up, authentically, to my relationship and communicating with Mr. Husband are the only ways that I can build and nurture deep intimacy in my relationship.

Eventually, I found Mr. Husband, and we got married (don't worry, there's a whole chapter ahead on our love story). But I had been married before and I know that having that wedding ring on my finger doesn't stop me from attention-seeking. In fact, it makes it worse. Being married meant that I could flirt excessively with whomever I wanted because I was married and it didn't mean anything, right? Wrong. It undermined my relationship with Mr. Ireland (my ex-husband) and it undermined my relationship to self (because I started to prefer this external validation to my own internal validation). I knew that I didn't want to go down this road with Mr. Husband, so I chose a different behavior.

Today, I have male acquaintances, but I really don't have male friends. Mr. Husband has female acquaintances, but he also doesn't have female friends. Here's why, and I truly believe this, in the heteronormative context, men and women can be acquaintances and can support one another but I don't think that we're capable of deep, sustainable, friendship. In my experience, somebody always develops romantic feelings. So, as Mr. Husband likes to say, "I don't have any business having some chick's phone number in my phone or meeting up with her for coffee." And this is generally true for me too. Unless we have some kind of actual business to discuss, I generally don't spend much time alone with men who aren't Mr. Husband and Mr. Husband generally doesn't spend much time alone with women who aren't me. I can acknowledge that this sounds extreme, and maybe it will make sense to you or maybe it won't. But, ask around, I bet it's more couples' M.O. than you think.

Jealousy

I think that jealousy is one of the most complex human emotions. I hate feeling jealous (just like I hate feeling threatened). In my ideal world, I would prefer it if I never, ever felt threatened or jealous. But, I'm a human and so these emotions are part of the experience. For me, jealousy is almost immediately followed by shame or guilt, so it's kind of like a one-two punch to the gut. But, over the years, I've learned that jealousy is just an emotion and as a human, it's generally expected that I will feel it. When the emotion of jealousy becomes too big, when it becomes the driving motive behind my behaviors and decisions, I know I am in trouble.

Today, when I experience jealousy, I can accept it. I can shed some light on it by talking about it. When I talk about jealousy, it's good for me to identify (1) how I'm feeling, and (2) what my needs are around it. Maybe that's some affection or attention from Mr. Husband; maybe it's to limit my own interaction or exposure with whomever sparked the feeling. If inquiring about someone makes me jealous, it's a good idea for me to just stop asking for "updates" about that person. I think there's a common misconception out there that we have to strive to have the best possible relations with every person we meet. I've discovered that for me, sometimes the best relationship I can have with a person is no relationship.

> For me, jealousy is almost immediately followed by shame or guilt, so it's kind of like a one-two punch to the gut.

Grandiosity

Grandiosity is a behavior that I used to put distance between me and other people. I would often engage in inappropriate grandiosity with people that I barely knew. For example, about a decade ago, I was dating Mr. Snowboarder for about a week before I went to Las Vegas. I knew that he loved bartending, had a bar in his apartment, and he was dying for a champagne stir to add to his bartending kit. I was in Las Vegas, partying it up, and I decided to swing by Tiffany and pick up a champagne stir (it had a snowflake on the end of it and was basically the perfect gift). When I returned to Portland and went on, maybe my fifth date with this guy, I pulled out this blue Tiffany box and gifted him this stir. It was so weird! Why would I do something like that? Because. Because I wanted him to think that I was a great gifter. I wanted him to think I was thoughtful. I wanted him to think

I wanted him to think that I was impulsive and some kind of manic-pixie-dream girl.

that I was impulsive and some kind of manic-pixie-dream girl. I wanted to manipulate his feelings about me by gifting him something opulent and outrageous.

When I looked back over my list, I had to take some time to accept and acknowledge that my past was Ok. That I did the best I could with what I had. But you know what, today I know better. And that is one of my favorite little mottos - "When we know better, we do better." I don't have to beat myself up with this stuff. I don't have to malign myself over relationships ruined by my constant demand for attention. It's Ok; it gave me something to look at and to learn about myself. And yes, those old patterns of behavior may have caused harm to others, but I don't have to use them to harm anyone else today. And that is truly glorious.

11

LET GO OR GET DRAGGED

In the last chapter, I asked you to make a list of the behaviors that you don't want to repeat in new relationships. I told you that by leaving those behaviors behind you would be making a living amends to both yourself and previous partners. Now, I'd like you to make a list of some of the behaviors that you want to practice in relationships. When you've done this list of new behaviors, I'd also like you to make a list of ideals for your future partner. Let's talk about behaviors that I wanted to bring to relationships first and then we can cover the ideals list.

Behaviors to bring to future relationships

Stay in today; i.e. let go or get dragged

This is a challenging one for me and it continues to be so. I am a planner. I like to have concrete goals and strategies for achieving them. This approach is well-suited for many aspects of my life, but—newsflash–interpersonal relationships is not one of them. This narrative that I have, of being able to plan, of arranging, is just an illusion. The reality – (and it is uncomfortable AF -) is that I don't really have control over much beyond my nose.

When I'm being honest, I can see that trying to control or take care of everything and everyone is manipulative. Because what I'm really trying to do manipulate the odds that everything will turn out how I'd like it to. One of the clearest examples of this in my life today is my relationship with Miss Stepdaughter.

Miss Stepdaughter is an absolute ray of sunshine. She is the best little angel-muffin that the universe could possibly have delivered to me. I love her. My only jobs are (1) to model for her what it looks like to be a grown-ass woman (her mom does this as well) and (2) to provide a stable and loving environment for her when she's home with us. But—omg there is always a but, amirite?—I have so many wants for her.

> The reality - and it is uncomfortable AF - is that I don't really have control over much beyond my nose.

There are so many things that I would love to plan for her: her extracurricular activities, academics, career, her future. Yet, almost all of her choices are completely out of my control. I do not get to insist that she play volleyball because she's tall and athletic and smart and because I think she should, so that she can go to a four-year college on a volleyball scholarship. I do not get to require that she attend this public school or that private one. I don't get to insist that she go to college. I get to advocate for her. I get to make suggestions and contribute ideas, but I don't get to arrange the outcomes for her simply because I think I'd like the way it would look. And that is, I think, the really funny thing about this. Sometimes I do all kinds of "work" to create something or make something come together, only to discover that when it does, I don't like the results.

It turns out, that when it comes to interpersonal relationships, the best course of action for me is to get comfortable with just being present for my life. I am to show up to my life as the woman I was intended to be. I am to be authentic. I am to communicate simply and honestly. I am supposed to be a human, so I will experience the full range of human emotions, and I am supposed to let go.

"Oh, but Heidi!!" you're saying, "What if I let go of trying to manage all these people and things and something bad happens?" It might. Letting go is possible because the work I did earlier—you know, the part where I asked you to find a power greater than yourself and to build a community of women—has allowed me to accept that there is a larger blueprint.

The concept of a "bigger plan" or a "blueprint" is complex and can be polarizing. I think that the cultural narrative around it implies that we get to see how all the pieces of this plan fit together, or that we get to see and understand the final product of the blueprint. But really, we don't. I don't always get to see how something in my life fits into the puzzle, and so it means that I don't always get closure. Sometimes, shit happens, and I learn something from it or later in life, I can see that one door closed and another door opened. But other times, shit happens, and it just hurts a lot and it's completely senseless. The point is, that I don't always get to understand an experience, and it's up to me to find a way to be Ok with that.

I really hate to admit it, but my life is infinitely better when I let go of trying to manage and manipulate my relationships. This means that I let go of trying to manage how people interpret what I do. I let go of trying to manage how someone will react to my feelings. This automatically leaves those big relationship fears (Is this guy Mr. Right? Will my relationship make it? Should I leave this job to pursue my passion project? Will Miss Step-Daughter go to college? Will Mr. Husband love me forever?) in the hands of the universe. In doing this, I've gained so much freedom from my obsession about my relationships that I found that I can show up authentically and be present in my life. What a gift.

Seek worth from within

So much of the pain that I have caused myself over the years has been in the pursuit of external validation. Even the process of writing this book has been bolstered by it. Every single time I send a link to a chapter out to a new beta reader, my mind races, "Will they like it?, Will they *love* it?, Will they love meeeee?" It's a pretty slippery slope over here, people! The truth is, occasionally, the drive for external validation still sneaks into my life. But does it rule my relationships anymore? Absolutely not.

I know it doesn't because early on Mr. Husband and I were having an argument about something and I was feeling uncomfortable and scared. Mr. Husband was still Mr. Boyfriend, but I knew that we were deeply committed to one another. This fight wasn't over anything deal-breaker-worthy. But I could not get over it. I needed to feel reassured by him that we were Ok. It felt like I was desperate for his validation. Like, I literally would have crawled into and curled up in his armpit forever if I could have. It felt like my self-worth depended on it. But I had done all the work that I've outlined here, and I could see this pattern and this feeling. It felt so familiar. And now that I was aware of it, it also felt gross. But I couldn't stop feeling this way.

So I took a step back and I said to myself, you know - every time I feel like this, I think that this is a Heidi B—Mr. Husband problem and it always takes a while for us to move through it. But what if this is not an HB—MH problem, what if this is about the relationship that I have with myself and my Higher Power (or my God, or the Universe, or whatever)? What if this is an HB—HP problem? What if this is about the fact that maybe something is off within me? What if this

> Sometimes, shit happens, and I learn something from it or later in life, I can see that one door closed and another door opened. But other times, shit happens, and it just hurts a lot and it's completely senseless. The point is, that I don't always get to understand an experience, and it's up to me to find a way to be Ok with that.

is really about how I relate to myself and how I relate to this power? What if, instead of seeking solace and affirmation in Mr. Husband, I turn inward, and I seek solace and affirmation from this guiding force in my life? If I did that, would it make me feel better? And if I felt better, would that change how I interacted with Mr. Husband? Would I be able to stop taking everything he did and said so personally? Would I be able to stop over-analyzing each interaction with him? Would I be able to stop obsessing over our relationship? I'll tell you what, I did. When I began to turn inward and to seek there, I became more confident, more self-assured, less frenzied. I leveled-up because I got some god-damned serenity in my life.

How, exactly, does one turn inward? This is a great question. I use prayer, meditation, and exercise. When I use these tools, I get tremendous clarity about what the next action is, or what my part is, or why I'm feeling frenzied. My very best prayer is often, "God, I'm fucked. Please help." I think this a great prayer because (1) it's honest and authentic, (2) it's short, and (3) it doesn't direct my God/Universe/Great Spirit/Higher Power to deliver any particular outcome or result.

Prayer does not require formality. You don't have to kneel, you don't have to say, "thy" or "thou," you don't have to memorize some bullshit that doesn't resonate with you. When you're done praying though, you do have to listen. That's where mediation comes it. If the prayer is the request, the meditation is the channel. Personally, I'm not great at just eyes closed, brain empty meditation. I prefer guided meditation. But I want to make a plug for exercise-based meditation. Because I know that there is something special about saying a quick prayer, lacing up your sneakers and then going for a trail run. I know that I've received clarity, communication, and encouragement from the Universe when I'm out there and I know other women have as well. So, if you are at all interested, give exercise-based meditation a shot.

> When I began to turn inward and to seek there, I became more confident, more self-assured, less frenzied. I leveled-up because I got some god-damned serenity in my life.

Finally, I like the idea of practicing gratitude as an action rather than just an acknowledged concept. Here's what I mean. Social media is great, and people are always posting on Instagram about how #blessed they are and about how much #gratitude they have. Sometimes it's kind of annoying, but other times it reminds me to get into action on my gratitude. I firmly believe that gratitude is about more than just standing around and proclaiming my thanks. I think that if I am truly grateful for something, then I must show my gratitude for that thing with my actions. For example, if I am grateful for my car, am I maintaining it? Is it clean? Do I drive it and insure it responsibly? If I am grateful for my health; am I taking care of my body, mind, and spirit? Am I exercising? Am I giving my body proper nutrition? You get the picture. Getting into the action of gratitude is a great way to break the cycle of obsession regardless of the object of obsession. Because I can just take a minute to identify my gratitude and then I can get into action expressing it (my car could always use a trip to the carwash, I can almost always do some tidying up of my home, there is always laundry to be done, etc).

Approach relationships from love rather than from fear, anxiety, or control

It is an entirely new concept for me to approach relationships from a place of love and trust rather than from a place of fear, anxiety, and control. I thought I was hard-wired to fear abandonment in my relationships. But having done this work, I know that if my relationship were to disintegrate, I would be Ok. It would cause me pain, but I'd survive. I have survived 100% of my worst days. Loving someone else requires accepting and loving myself first. It requires being willing to share that whole self with someone else - not just the parts I like or that I think they'll like. I've learned that if I am authentic and vulnerable and someone doesn't like that, it's Ok. They just can't roll with me.

> I thought I was hard-wired to fear abandonment in my relationships.

I can't tell you how many times I had read about this concept in self-help books. But I had to actually try to live it to believe that it was true. I could read "If you're totally you and he's not into that, then he's not for you" a million times, but I couldn't accept it. Until I got there. Until I got to a place where I loved myself, where I knew myself, where I believed that I was the baddest bitch in the room. Only then did I understand that he (that boyfriend, that crush, that husband) could walk away and I'd be Ok. When I had clarity around that, then it began to feel like I had nothing left to lose. I began to approach my relationships loving myself. And then, miraculously, I began to experience love in my relationships.

Today that looks like accepting myself and accepting Mr. Husband, meeting one another where we're at, and making a commitment to grow together from there. When I approach my relationships in fear, I'm always trying to control, manipulate, or change the other person. I don't believe that we can be fully in fear and fully in love at the same time. So I choose to be in love. I choose to accept myself and to accept Mr. Husband.

Ideal Qualities List

Now you've got an idea of what some of my new behaviors for future relationships looked like. Once I had these two lists (behaviors to kick to the curb and behaviors I'd like to bring with me) I had to make one final list (I know—so many lists!): a list of the characteristics or qualities for an ideal partner for me. This one is actually pretty fun!

I'd like you to list all the qualities that you'd find attractive in a partner. I want you to do this now, while you're still single, because in the heat of the moment - when we are totally hot for someone- it's too easy to overlook qualities that are missing from Mr. Hottie because we are so busy staring deep into his eyes. If your list is already made, you can hit up Mr. Hottie for a few dates, get to know him, gather some information and then compare it to your list. Long story short, trust me, it's a more objective assessment if you make the list today than if you make it after your first date with Mr. Hottie.

Your list can be as extensive or concise as you find necessary, and I don't want you to use this list to mercilessly rule out suitors. But I want you to have it, so you can see how each guy stacks up to your recipe for the perfect partner. Some examples of qualities for this list include; honest, outdoorsy, funny/can make me laugh, empathetic, good listener, gainfully employed, self-supporting, loves dogs, etc. Get your list dialed in and know that as long as it is a quality that is authentic for you, it should go on there. Don't add qualities to the list because you think other people think they are important. This is your recipe for the perfect partner, not theirs - you know my list does not have outdoorsy on it!

Now for the twist: because it's a list for your partner, but it's also a list for you. So, if you value honesty in a partner, you need to be sure that you are prioritizing honesty in your life. If you value financial security in a partner, your own financial house better be in order. If your ideal partner is a travel-lover, you better pack that bag, girl! The point is, that when it comes to this stuff, we attract what we put out there. And if you are committed to living a life based on these principles/ideals, you are more likely to find a partner who is as well.

After all this work you've done, you know so much more about yourself and your dating patterns than you did when we started. Congratulations! Some people never take the time to look at this stuff and to learn from it, but you did! I am so excited to have walked you through it and I feel truly #blessed to have been trusted with your process. If you followed the suggestions outlined here, it's been a minute since you dated. But now you're ready to start dating and you know I have some thoughts on that. The next chapter, Chapter 12, outlines some good guidelines for dipping that toe back into the dating pool. It will surely be a different experience, but remember, we don't do this alone!

Don't add qualities to the list because you think other people think they are important. This is your recipe for the perfect partner, not theirs.

12

SWIMMING WITH THE SHARKS

You've finished up all this work and you're ready to start dating again. I know I was. I was chomping at the bit to get out there, practice all these new things, and to fall in love. Finally, I was ready to find a deep and meaningful love, this time everything would be so much different.

Let me tell you how it went down. Prior to this journey of self-discovery, I had been flirting with this guy who was an artist and had a silk-screening company -for custom order t-shirts and hoodies and stuff. Right before I finished, I had an occasion to see him (a custom sweatshirt order for a girlfriend). It was nice and he was cute. I had decided, "you know, when I'm ready to date, I'm gonna ask this guy out." So when Ms. Warrior Spirit gave me a little key and said, "Ok, Heidi, you're off lockdown you can start dating again," the first thing I did was text Mr. T-Shirt to see if he wanted to go out.

After a little flirting via text, I checked his availability boxes, (1) he was single and (2) he lived just outside of Portland, so he wasn't long distance. We decided to meet at a bar near my house for a few drinks. Now, you know I don't drink, so it was Diet Coke and soda water for me. But Mr. T-Shirt had a few drinks. We bopped back to my house, we made out and we had sex. Eventually, I fell asleep and he passed out. When I woke up the next morning, I was so mortified. I thought that my days of this kind of shame were squarely behind me, I didn't drink anymore, I had spent months doing all this work! How could I have made such a bad decision, bringing this guy home!?!?

After he left, I called Ms. Warrior Spirit and I cried. Like super-hard. I was in a total shame spiral, I was embarrassed, I felt sick to my stomach, it was awful. But Ms. Warrior Spirit asked me to step out of the shame-spiral, to take a deep breath and to consider how available this guy might really be. Of all the things to bring to my attention, the question of availability was the first on her list. And do you know why? Because she knew about my pattern of attraction to unavailable men and she was holding me accountable to some different behavior.

As I thought about it, an answer that I didn't want to be the answer came to me. This guy wasn't emotionally available. He wasn't ready to date for whatever reason. I was so mad - I did all this work and I wanted the first guy that I dated to be *the guy*!! Mr. T-Shirt called me later that evening and basically told me as much himself. He let me know that he had been through a pretty rough breakup and was staying with his parents while he was trying to get back on his feet.

I processed this a little bit with Ms. Warrior Spirit, and she encouraged me to really hear his unavailability. I didn't want to. I was being stubborn. But she suggested that I delete his number from my phone and that I unfriend him on social media and stuff. So, I did. And I kind of, like, set him down and walked away from him. And by the end of the week, I wasn't even pissed off about it. This was the first time that chaos, drama, and unavailability had come knocking at my door and I had decided not to answer.

I bounced back from the Mr. T-Shirt incident and I figured that I would find Mr. Right on Tinder. I set up my profile, I added a cutie pic, and I was ready. I started chatting with a guy and I met him at a park where he cooked me dinner (which sounds even more bizarre than it was in real life) and then he invited me back to his place. I decided that I wanted to go.

We had been making out a little and he was ratcheting up the pressure for us to head to the bone-zone. But I was clear, I didn't want to, and I told him as much. "C'mon, what's the worst that could happen?" I couldn't believe this jackass. What's the worst that could happen?!?! "Oh, I don't know, maybe you give me some kind of STD, or maybe I get pregnant, or maybe you fuck me and then murder me and then chop me into a million little pieces and stuff me in an oil drum!!" I shouted at him as I gathered my shit up and walked out the door.

> I was so mad - I did all this work and I wanted the first guy that I dated to be *the guy*!!

And again, I set this guy aside (I didn't call, or text and I didn't feel compelled to return his calls or texts) and after about a week I was over him. I wasn't getting sucked into dating guys who were unavailable or with whom I didn't see eye to eye. Oh my god, you guys! This was a fucking miraculous event. Here, I had been on a date with a guy that had treated me like shit and instead of becoming obsessed with him and going all in on some drama and chaos, I fucking walked away from him. What. Was. Happening???

I had mixed feelings about it all. Going back to dating was such an emotional roller-coaster; I felt entitled to find love and to find it five minutes ago! But at the same time, I was using all the information I had about myself and my patterns to evaluate and assess my behaviors. I was beginning to pick up some new tools. I was beginning to behave differently, which was tremendously satisfying. I was moving into a space where I could feel the pain of engaging in that old behavior and I decided the price was more than I was willing to pay. So, I did something different, something new, and I walked away. It was amazing to honor my truth and my authenticity; to know that these guys weren't good or bad, they just weren't right for me. But even more than that, to know that I didn't need them to be Ok. I'm a bad bitch, and that's true whether I'm single or dating or engaged or married or divorced or married again. I assessed what was going on, I made a new choice, and I held my head high.

After these incidents, I got four suggestions about dating that I think are valuable and that I want to pass on to you. I know you're not gonna like them, I didn't when I heard them either. But call it timing, call it kismet, call it good orderly direction, I used them when I started to date Mr. Husband and he's the only man that I ever tested them on.

Going back to dating was such an emotional roller-coaster; I felt entitled to find love and to find it 5 minutes ago!

You use the information that you get from going on a date with someone to assess their suitability as a partner to you.

No Kissing until the 4th Date

The point of dating is to actually get to know someone. To go out and learn some things about someone else and to share some things about yourself. To go home and think about how you might feel about the things you learned about that person. To consider whether or not you and that person actually get along, and to determine if you'd like to see that person again. You use the information that you get from going on a date with someone to assess their suitability as a partner to you. If you think it's a thumbs up, you go on another date. If you'd rather organize your closet than go share a burger with this guy, it's probably a hard pass; assuming that it's the guy, not the shared burger, that's the problem.

If you decide to go on the second date, you get to learn even more information about this person. After the date is over, you get to reassess and re-evaluate your compatibility with them. And you get to make another decision about whether you'd like to see them again. The point is, at any stage in this information gathering process, you get to change your mind. You are always allowed to reassess and re-evaluate. But reassessing and re-evaluating gets harder for me once things get physical.

The no-kissing-before-the-fourth-date suggestion helped to keep me from diving right into getting physical with someone before I knew anything about them (which was definitely an old pattern of behavior for me, see Mr. T-Shirt). But it really doesn't take that long to go on four dates. Like seriously, if you were that hot for each other you could easily go on four dates within a week. So, there's that. And for me, once I've gotten physical with someone, it's harder for me to see the red flags, or to acknowledge that he and I don't see eye to eye. Before you start making out with this guy, I want you to go on a few dates with him, to get some information about him, and to compare that information to the ideals list that you made in the last chapter. I guarantee you, that it will be easier to honestly assess how he measures up to that ideals list if you haven't been kissing him than it will be if you have.

Finally, this is a good litmus test for a partner's boundaries. Suggesting that you wait until the 4th date before getting physical is a very reasonable request. Giving you a lot of grief about this (like teasing you or making fun) or pushing back on it hard (like negotiating with you about which date it should be) gives you some information about this person already. It indicates that he's not capable of respecting your boundaries and it's a red flag. A man who doesn't agree with this suggestion but respects your boundaries would likely just say something like, "I've had a nice time getting to know you, but I just don't think we are a good match," and would walk away with grace and dignity. Just know, if he can't handle this request, then he can't handle you.

I used this suggestion with Mr. Husband, and I think it has something to do with why I will always remember our first kiss. Mr. Husband and I went on a dinner date, then we went on a baseball game date, then we went on another dinner date, and finally we went on a dinner date with a walk around the waterfront in Portland. As we were bee-bopping down the west side we were holding hands and we were both super aware that we were on our fourth date. It was summertime and there was an orchestra set up on the waterfront. As the orchestra played, a fireworks display started. Mr. Husband hugged me from behind and I turned around to look at him, and our eyes met, and we kissed. Under the fireworks, accompanied by an orchestra! It was magic.

Share your story with him, but not all of it on the first date

This is not about being inauthentic or dishonest. It's about sharing your story in an appropriate way. Look, I used to be awful at this one. I love being the center of attention and I had a knack for making my story sound tragic. I was never, ever one to hold this back. And I found that, especially when I was drinking, I was suddenly airing every single tiny detail of my life to some guy I had just met. You know I am all about authenticity and vulnerability, but sharing my story at this level of detail with some dude I'd just met in a bar in the hopes that he would fall in love with me was not authentic, it was inappropriate and manipulative. I'm sharing all the gory details of my life with you, but I'm not trying to make you fall for me. I want my story to help you dig around your story so that you can learn something new about yourself.

> Secure intimacy develops over time, so, once you've established your date as someone that you can trust, it makes sense to begin to share with him at whatever level of detail you are comfortable.

Secure intimacy develops over time, so once you've established your date as someone that you can trust, it makes sense to begin to share with him at whatever level of detail you are comfortable. This might be after your third date, it might be after your twentieth date, but the point is, when you're ready you'll be able to say something like, "I wanna tell you the full story on my experience growing up in Iowa…" or "My dad died when I was 28, and our relationship was really complex. Can I tell you more about it?"

His friends are his friends, not yours

This is one that I never would have thought of on my own. But especially when I was obsessed with being the cool girl, I always prioritized the importance of winning over his friends. It used to matter so much to me that his friends thought I was the best girlfriend ever. I can remember feeling like I needed his friends to think, "Damn, I wish my girlfriend were that cool." Oh, it's always about the winning for me. So, here's the thing, now that you've done this work, (1) it doesn't matter what his friends think of you - you're not dating them, you're dating him, and (2) his friends should be his friends, not yours!

This suggestion is really about avoiding the transitive properties of friends. Or the presumption that because you like him and his friends also like him, that his friends will like you. I'm not saying that they won't. I'm just saying that he has probably put years of time and energy into creating these sustained friendships. If you've only been dating him for three months and you've only hung out with his friends a few times just don't mistake their politeness for friendship. All to say, that if you and he hit a rocky bump, expect that he'll be talking to them about it. And you'll be talking to all those girlfriends you spent the last few months making about it. If you and he hit a rocky patch after three months of dating, it would be wildly inappropriate for you to go to his friends to talk about it. You should process shit with your girlfriends, and he should process shit with his guy-friends. End of story.

No sex or overnight trips until you are exclusive

Finally, this one. It's along the same lines as no kissing until after the fourth date, but it's leveled-up. And it usually sends the women I've worked with reeling. Because you've spent all this time doing this work, you haven't been talking to men, you're going to wait until the fourth date to kiss, and now I'm asking you to wait until you're exclusive to head to the bone-zone (I'm sorry, I know with that phrase, but I just can't stop!) or to overnight with this guy. Remember, all the things I've outlined here are just suggestions and personally, I think you should take them all. But with this one, if you can't do both, I think it's more important that you wait to have sex with him until you know you are exclusive.

But why, Heidi? Nobody waits to fuck until they are exclusive! It's 2019, not 1889. Because getting physical can really cloud our judgement about the suitability of a partner, that's why. And I want you to have experienced this guy's full range of emotion before you start sleeping with him. I want you to have had a disagreement with him, I want you to have seen him

Because when you start sleeping with him, I want you to have seen him as his true, human self. Not just his dating profile.

angry, I want you to have seen him disappointed. Why? Because when you start sleeping with him, I want you to have seen him as his true, human self. Not just as his dating profile. I don't want you to find yourself head over heels for a guy and totally physically into him, only to discover that when he is   angry,   it   scares   you.

It's like imagine you're dating Mr. Handy. And he buys something at Home Depot, but it's the wrong wrench size (or whatever tool thing fits). And you go with him to return it and the customer service agent is like, "Well, do you have your receipt? Oh, you don't. Ok, can you verify that this was your transaction…" you know, whatever. And you're watching him get frustrated. And you can relate, because this is annoying. But then, he loses his shit and he just completely unloads on this customer service agent. "THIS IS BULLSHIT!! I WANNA SPEAK TO YOUR MANAGER! WHERE'S THE FUCKING GOD-DAMNED MANAGER OF THIS SHIT-HOLE? YOU MUST BE A MISERABLE FUCKING LOSER TO WORK IN THIS JOINT. YOU'RE PARENTS MUST BE

If you and he hit a rocky patch after 3 months of dating, it would be wildly inappropriate for you to go to his friends to talk about it.

REAAAAAL PROUD OF YOU!!" and on and on, just berating this customer service agent.

I'm not saying that you need to leave this guy. I'm just saying, I want you to have seen him have this kind of meltdown before you start sleeping with him. Because I think it's important for us to have this kind of information about our partners' behavior before we get physically attached. Because for some women, witnessing this would be extremely uncomfortable and would be a deal-breaker, and for others this would be no big deal. Regardless, in an ideal situation, you will have seen your partner angry, fearful, sad, or all three before you become exclusive with him and start sleeping with him. Because if your partner's fear, anger, or sadness manifests in some kind of behavior that is completely unacceptable to you, it will be easier to reassess your compatibility (and by extension, exclusivity) with him, if you haven't already gotten physical.

Maintenance

I would suggest taking some time to check back in on patterns pretty regularly. You did all the work to find them, you may as well see if you're still engaging in them, right? So, what does that look like? As you start dating, just take a minute before you go to bed to review your day. Did you engage in any of those old behaviors? If you did, look at it with a narrower lens, what was it about the interaction that made you panic and pick up those old "first-strike" tools? If you could do it differently, what would you do instead? If you're into writing, write this -ish down. If you're not, no big, I think that just having a good mental recap is enough.

But understand this, you're a different woman than you were when you started this, so it's entirely possible that you won't be attracted to the men that you were flirting with when you hit the pause button on dating.

Also, some of those guys that you were talking to when you started this - you know - the guys you had to put on hold? They'll be re-surfacing when they hear that you're dating again. But understand this, you're a different woman than you were when you started, so it's entirely possible that you won't be attracted to the men that you were flirting with when you hit the pause button on dating. And please do not fucking forget that for a lot of these guys, you already have all the information you need. If he used to make you feel like shit when you went out, he probably still will. Don't waste your precious time on him.

Finally, dating is supposed to be fun. So, don't take any of it too seriously. Relax and enjoy the food, the coffee, the activity, the company and the opportunity to both meet someone new and to share a part of yourself with that person. Trust me, the universe didn't bring you all this way, only to drop you on your ass. Let go of the reigns and let the universe deliver the experience to you!

13

MR. HUSBAND, A LOVE STORY

Mr. Husband and I met in 2012. We were both attending the same meetings in a twelve-step program. We didn't start dating until two years later, in September of 2014; I had just about three years of sobriety and he had two years. I had taken a year off dating to do the work I've outlined here (it really did take me eleven months to complete it all). Mr. Husband had followed his sponsor's advice and had abstained from dating in order to focus on his sobriety.

There are pros and cons to dating someone in recovery (similar lifestyle, shared commitment to seeking a spiritual way of life, egomania, narcissism, the obsession of the untreated alcoholic brain, and the potential for relapse). It's suggested that people in early sobriety (less than 12 months sober) refrain from dating, and instead take the first year to get to know themselves. By the time I got sober, I had been using alcohol to numb and change my feelings for 16 years. In early sobriety, I struggled to even identify how I was feeling in real time. I was not an available partner. So, if you are out bopping along and you swipe right on a guy who tells you he's just started exploring getting sober, let him go!

Mr. Husband and I went out on two quasi-dates, before we finally decided we were dating. We went to coffee. I remember, because I had just gotten the "go-ahead" to date, but I was unsure as to whether or not this coffee date was really a date. Mr. Husband and I each paid for our own coffee. We sat at the coffee bar and we chatted about all kinds of stuff. I found out that Mr. Husband had been a writer for an awesome local newspaper and that he had gone to law school for a few years. He had moved to Manhattan on September 10th, 2001 and had planned to clerk or intern with a law firm in the city. And then. September 11th. Everything changed. Mr. Husband eventually wrote a fucking amazing article on what it was like to move to NYC the day before the 9/11 attacks. About how, in the aftermath, it was tough to deliver resumes in large brown envelopes to prestigious law firms because there were reports of anthrax being delivered the same way. About how, it turned out, he wouldn't be interning there after all. Mr. Husband was funny, he was like, I know 9/11 wasn't about me, but it seemed like a pretty good sign from the universe that I didn't belong in Manhattan. We laughed and flirted a little and the time just flew by. We parted ways, maybe with a hug, but it could have been a high-five.

> He had a great palette. I was impressed; because as a true-blue Midwesterner, the only seasoning I was familiar with was salt.

A couple of months passed. Then in July, I got a phone call from Mr. Husband. Did I want to meet him from dinner? I did. We met at a spot called Son of a Biscuit, a counter-service, fried-chicken joint. We ordered and ate. When we finished up, we took a walk around the neighborhood and I learned more about him. He had a seven-year-old daughter that he loved more than anything. He was sad because she wasn't able to spend his birthday with him that year. He had worked in the wine industry and he had nearly attended a fancy pants gastronomy school in Europe. He loved food. He had a great palette. I was impressed because as a true-blue Midwesterner, the only seasoning I was familiar with was salt. I would go to restaurants in Portland and review the menu, only to blush with embarrassment. I certainly knew the word thyme and what it meant, but I had no idea of how it would affect the flavor of my food.

We parted ways and I thought to myself, "was that a date? Was I just on a date with Mr. Husband?" I looked at what I was wearing. Cutoff shorts and a button-down shirt. I certainly wasn't dressed for a date. I hadn't done my make-up because when I had accepted the invitation, I hadn't considered it a date. But this felt like a date. And Mr. Husband was interesting, and he was cute! I call this my ninja-date with Mr. Husband, because to me it came as a surprise. He remembers it a little differently. He recalls, very distinctly, that he was clear about asking me out. He knows that when he called, he'd told me that he had enjoyed spending time with me and wanted to spend more time together. Funny how two people can recall the same event so differently.

> Funny how two people can recall the same event so differently.

I had been planning a trip with some friends to go see a Seattle Mariners baseball game. I am not crazy about baseball on tv, but I love seeing a baseball game in person. I love the summer sun, I love the fresh cut grass, I love watching the outfielders feign interest when they are just kind of hanging, out there. I love the concessions, I love a Diet Coke, I love that it takes all afternoon. I just love it. So, I purchased a block of tickets and started recruiting people to take a road trip to Seattle for a game. I decided to invite Mr. Husband. Mr. Husband is a serious baseball fan. He loves the stats, the trading, the players, the espionage. I planned to drive and each seat in my car was full. Until the night before the game, one by one, friends texted to say that actually they couldn't make it. That was fine, I was going to this game, come hell or high-water.

The next day, I went to go pick up Mr. Husband. I met him at a coffee shop. I let him know it would just be him and me in the car. He turned green. Later he told me, he nearly died from anxiety. But he got in my car. And we spent two hours driving to Seattle, getting to know one another. He was a good listener, he listened as I filled him in on the perils of online dating and the details of a slew of bad dates I had recently been on (including Mr. What's-the-worst-that-can-happen). We discussed the dying art of letter writing and how important it is to both of us. We stopped along the way to get gas for the car. We got out and took a selfie - he'd never taken one before! He put his arm around my waist, his hand lingered when we had finished our pose. And then I knew: Mr. Husband was into me! And I was fucking seriously into him too!

Mr. Husband was headed to New Hampshire to visit his parents. But he started texting me while he was gone and a few days later, I received a postcard from him. And then another. Mr. Husband had been listening when I told him I loved the written word! And he texted me a picture of a bear that was "taking a selfie," and he made me laugh. So we decided that we should go out on a proper date when he returned.

Mr. Husband picked me up at my place and he brought me flowers (swoon). We went to dinner and then settled into a dessert spot. I let him know the suggestions that I had been given about dating. He heard me, and we agreed that we would date with them in mind. "But wait," I said, "we went to coffee a long time ago, and then we had our ninja date, and then we went to the baseball game. So what number date is this?" Because you know I wanted to get to that fourth date!! We agreed that we would consider this dinner date our second date - lumping all the other excursions together as one.

The next week, Mr. Husband and I went on another date where we ate sushi and went to a twelve-step meeting together. It was lovely. I continued to get information about him, and I had the opportunity to assess and reassess our compatibility. I liked him and I was having fun. Finally, Mr. Husband and I had our fourth date—you already heard about this in the last chapter. We had a magical first kiss that was accompanied by an orchestra, fireworks, and the warm autumn breeze.

Mr. Husband and I continued to date, and we committed to exclusivity. We took a weekend trip to Astoria, OR. We hit up a farmer's market, we got massages during the day. We found a quarter arcade, where we discussed the finer points of the movie *Ghost*. And I insisted that Mr. Husband promise me that he wouldn't get murdered like Patrick Swayze did. We had fun and we kept having fun.

Mr. Husband and I dated for a little more than a year before we moved in together. In that time there was a lot of back and forth between his place and mine. It was challenging. I'll always be grateful for it though, because it has given me a ton of compassion for his kiddo, who splits her time between our home and her mom's. I know how hard it was to haul my shit back and forth between his place and mine. How it felt like I was always kind of living out of my car. How it became easier to just have a hair-straightener at both places. And I was doing it as a 35-year-old woman. How these little boos in blended families do that week in and week out and don't completely lose their shit is beyond me.

One day, Mr. Husband texted me, "Heidi, can I pick up any groceries for your place?" Before giving it a second thought, I fired off a text, "carrots, hummus, milk, cheerios, cheese." As soon as I sent it; I felt so vulnerable! Jesus Heidi!! Why would you do that? What will he think?!?! It's amazing how exposed being deeply in love with Mr. Husband made me feel sometimes. My instinct, my old behavior, was to become completely self-sufficient in my relationship. But I ran this idea by a few people and got some great advice, "Heidi," they said. "Don't rob Mr. Husband of the opportunity to show up for you." They reminded me, it's impossible to be in partnership with someone when you don't allow the other person the space to show up, to support you, to cheerlead you, to help you. It was important for me to learn how to ask my partner to help me. That might not be something you

> It's impossible to be in partnership with someone when you don't allow the other person the space to show-up, to support you, to cheerlead you, to help you.

struggle with, but if it is, I want you to know that it's possible to be a strong independent woman and to ask for help. In fact, it's more than possible, it's necessary in order to build reciprocal friendships and relationships.

Mr. Husband and I both feel strongly about one thing: we believe that fear and love are two sides of the same coin. That I can choose to be in fear, or I can choose to be in love, but it is rare, if not impossible, to be in both. Early on, we started checking in with one another about how fearful we were feeling (I think it was the best way for us to gauge and share our level of comfort with the vulnerability we were each experiencing). Shortly after the grocery-list incident, he and I were watching a Kevin Hart comedy special on my couch. He was sitting up, I was laying on the couch, my head in his lap. He said to me, "Heidi, where is your fear level at, today?" And I looked up at him, I smiled, and I said, "I think I've moved out of fear and into love." And he said, "me too." And honestly, I felt so safe. We had been dating for about four months at that stage.

Mr. Husband and I got married in June of 2018. That we got married at all is ironic; when I met him, I promised him, I would never marry him. As we dated and our lives became more deeply entwined, we decided that getting married was about more than just a piece of paper. We both wanted the opportunity to make a commitment to one another in front of our friends, our family and universal spirit.

We went to Maui for our honeymoon and we spent the majority of the trip in Hana, a remote and beautiful spot on the island. We had an ocean-front bungalow with an eastern exposure. The sun rose on us while we were still in bed, and as we slept, we could hear the power of the elements as the waves crashed on the rocks and the wind whipped around. Liminal space is the space between the "what was" and the "next." And we spent time in the liminality - the space between the transition from boyfriend and girlfriend to husband and wife. I never anticipated that it would be so beautiful.

I have come to understand that our relationship is resilient and that it can withstand all the emotions and humanness we each bring to it. That short of physical violence and infidelity (both of which are extremely unlikely), I am committed to growing together with Mr. Husband. Today, that means that I am honest with him when I don't want to be, that I share my humanness with him when it's hard. It means that when shit is going sideways for him, I ask him questions about it instead of trying to rush to a solution and fix it for him. These new behaviors are so important because they are the path to deep intimacy and a sustainable relationship. I don't practice them perfectly, and I don't expect you to either. The point is, that we practice. We keep showing up, we keep trying something that feels uncomfortable at first and we keep growing.

Final thoughts

You've purchased this workbook and so, as you know, you can do whatever you want with it. You can use it as a coaster. You can light your money on fire by tossing it in your fireplace. Or you can use it. I can't tell you how many guides and books I have hanging around that I didn't ever use. And some of them I still can't muster any willingness to use. Generally, my pattern is: (1) experience pain/discomfort (2) purchase book with proven solution to

Liminal space is the space between the "what was" and the "next."

the specific pain or discomfort that I'm experiencing (3) open book and start reading (4) laugh at funny anecdotes (5) get to an exercise (6) close book and put it back on the shelf, effectively kissing my money goodbye.

My hope is that you use this guide and that you do the exercises in the order they have been suggested. Once you've done the exercises and built the tools, you can use them at any time and in any order you please.

Also, do what you can to manage your expectations. It took me 11 months to do this work. Honestly, I thought it would only take me about 30 days, which is why I agreed to do it in the first place. And, once I was finished, I still went on some pretty bad dates. Although, to my credit, I did not become involved with any of those bad apples. The universe did not deliver me the love of my life on a silver platter the minute I set down the pencil. But the universe did deliver. The man that I share my life with today is the most incredible being in the solar system, in the universe, in my heart. I am human and he is human, but what we share—honesty, tolerance, communication, and a deep commitment to building intimacy and trust, it is the stuff that I always thought was out of reach. The stuff that I thought was for other people but not for me. I am delighted to know that it was always there for me, I just had to get out of my own way to receive it.

NAME	YOUR AGE	SUMMARY OF THE RELATIONSHIP – HIGHLIGHTS AND LOWLIGHTS	IN WHAT WAY DID THIS RELATIONSHIP AFFECT ME?	IS THIS RELATIONSHIPPART OF, OR REFLECTIVE OF, A LARGER PATTERN?	WHAT WAS YOUR PART IN THE CHAOS/DRAMA OF THIS

NAME	YOUR AGE	SUMMARY OF THE RELATIONSHIP – HIGHLIGHTS AND LOWLIGHTS	IN WHAT WAY DID THIS RELATIONSHIP AFFECT ME?	IS THIS RELATIONSHIP PART OF, OR REFLECTIVE OF, A LARGER PATTERN?	WHAT WAS YOUR PART IN THE CHAOS/DRAMA OF THIS

NAME	YOUR AGE	SUMMARY OF THE RELATIONSHIP – HIGHLIGHTS AND LOWLIGHTS	IN WHAT WAY DID THIS RELATIONSHIP AFFECT ME?	IS THIS RELATIONSHIP/PART OF, OR REFLECTIVE OF, A LARGER PATTERN?	WHAT WAS YOUR PART IN THE CHAOS/DRAMA OF THIS

NAME	YOUR AGE	SUMMARY OF THE RELATIONSHIP -- HIGHLIGHTS AND LOWLIGHTS	IN WHAT WAY DID THIS RELATIONSHIP AFFECT ME?	IS THIS RELATIONSHIP PART OF, OR REFLECTIVE OF, A LARGER PATTERN?	WHAT WAS YOUR PART IN THE CHAOS/DRAMA OF THIS

NAME	YOUR AGE	SUMMARY OF THE RELATIONSHIP -- HIGHLIGHTS AND LOWLIGHTS	IN WHAT WAY DID THIS RELATIONSHIP AFFECT ME?	IS THIS RELATIONSHIP/PART OF, OR REFLECTIVE OF, A LARGER PATTERN?	WHAT WAS YOUR PART IN THE CHAOS/DRAMA OF THIS

NAME	YOUR AGE	SUMMARY OF THE RELATIONSHIP -- HIGHLIGHTS AND LOWLIGHTS	IN WHAT WAY DID THIS RELATIONSHIP AFFECT ME?	IS THIS RELATIONSHIPPA RT OF, OR REFLECTIVE OF, A LARGER PATTERN?	WHAT WAS YOUR PART IN THE CHAOS/DRAMA OF THIS

FEARS LIST

I AM	I DESIRE

BEHAVIORS YOU **DON'T WANT**
TO BRING TO NEW RELATIONSHIPS

BEHAVIORS YOU WANT TO
BRING TO NEW RELATIONSHIPS

IDEAL QUALITIES LIST

COACHING WITH HEIDI

It is absolutely my calling in life to take other women through the work I've outlined in this book. If you're tired of fucking randos, you're ready for a relationship, and you're ready to do some work, then we should talk about doing this work together. You can reach out to me directly at heidi@heidibcoaching.com or
www.heidibcoaching.com

ABOUT THE AUTHOR

Heidi Busche Jassmond lives in Portland, OR with her loving husband, Jeff, the crazy-smart-amazing, Ms. Stepdaughter, and their two dogs, Henri and Lemon. You can always catch more of Heidi by listening to All Gold Everything, a podcast she co-hosts with The Real Sandy J, about pop-culture, love, and relationships.

Made in the
USA
Columbia, SC